# A Guide to Writing & Presenting in Music Therapy

by Kenneth Aigen

Barcelona
PUBLISHERS

ISBN 1-891278-18-5

2 4 6 8 9 7 5 3 1

Distributed throughout the world by:
Barcelona Publishers
4 White Brook Road
Gilsum NH 03448
Tel: 603-357-0236 Fax: 603-357-2073
Website: www.barcelonapublishers.com
SAN 298-6299

*We are all writers and readers as well as communicators, with the need at times to please and satisfy ourselves . . . with the clear and almost perfect thought.*

—Roger Angell, Foreword to *The Elements of Style*

# Acknowledgments

I would like to thank two wonderful communicators in music therapy with whom I have had the privilege of working for many years, Florence Tyson and Clive Robbins. Florence did not have much involvement with my scholarly writings but she did teach me a very important skill: how to write a business letter with clarity and succinctness. Although I had to rewrite letters for her many times, I never did so with resentment because whenever we had disagreements about a grammatical construction or a particular word usage, further investigation on my part revealed that she was always correct.

Clive is a communicative inspiration to all who hear him speak and read his writings. The joy he takes in putting words to seemingly ineffable music therapy experiences reminds me of a sculptor working his stone. Each section of the whole is equally important and he has taught me that the care one takes in one's writing should reflect the esteem in which one holds the experience and people one is writing about.

My gratitude also goes to the Mid-Atlantic Region of the American Music Therapy Association. The region accepted my proposal for a Continuing Music Therapy Education course on the topic "Communicating with Colleagues" at its conference in Williamsburg, Virginia, during the spring of 2001, and the contents of that course developed into this publication.

Kenneth Bruscia read and commented upon a draft of this publication and provided suggestions that were essential in making it more complete and easier to read. Considering the contributions to the development of the music therapy profession made by his own publications, there is no person better suited than Ken to help shape a publication such as the present one. I am extraordinarily grateful for his guidance.

Thanks to my father, Mitchell Aigen, who gave me my first copy of Strunk & White's book *The Elements of Style* and to whom I owe the notion that clarity in writing reflects clarity of thought.

# Contents

# Tables



# Examples

# Preface

Many of the considerations entailed in developing professional presentations and publications revolve around two central questions: What do you want to say? And, How do you want to say it? In essence, this publication is an elaboration of these questions.

In passing along my thoughts on this topic, it is relevant to mention my belief that professional communications are a form of advocacy and are not merely informational. As scholar-clinicians, each of us has a particular point of view on clinical work, the nature of theory, and the types of interventions and treatment frameworks which are most beneficial to clients. When we communicate with colleagues, we organize and present information in a way to convince them of the value of these precepts and practices.

This contrasts with the traditional notion of professional communications drawn from the scientific model. This view holds that the scholar is a dispassionate gatherer and disseminator of information without personal investment in it. In this model, the scholar or professional presents objective data, evidence, or information and the audience draws conclusions from them. In contrast, my view on professional communications is influenced by my perspective on qualitative research: all knowledge claims are framed by their contexts which are variable; value neutrality in research and other scholarly or professional activities does not exist; and there is no such thing as a neutral voice in writing.

That much said, in this book I am speaking to all music therapists, regardless of the type of research, theory, or clinical work with which you are aligned. Many of the components of effective professional communications transcend these types of differences because they are focused upon sharpening your own perceptions about the form and structure of your communications and bringing these in line with your content. The type of thinking engaged in this activity, for the most part, is not specific to any particular type of clinical or conceptual content.

In the advocacy model of communications it is acknowledged that writers and presenters have agendas. We apply scholarly standards to our communications by being forthcoming about these agendas, not by ignoring them. My agenda in the present publication is a simple one: to advance the level of understanding and practice in the profession of music therapy by assisting music therapists in the formulation of their professional communications. The process of organizing our various talks and publications for dissemination forces us to enhance and bring clarity to the material constituting them. When we have some insight into the various types of communications and their functions, we can choose those forms best suited to the content of our message.

One caveat: The assertions and observations in this book reflect my 20 years of experience as a music therapist with 10 of those years consisting primarily of research, writing, presenting, and editing activities. However, they are impressions gleaned from my general experience rather than outcomes of specific scholarly investigations and should be taken as such.

# A Guide to Writing & Presenting in Music Therapy

## CHAPTER I

# Types of Professional Communications

### Communications Addressed in this Publication

The term "professional communications" refers to a potentially wide variety of types of publications and talks. For the purposes of this book, I am considering primarily those forms of professional communications which are directed to music therapy colleagues, subject to some type of peer review—whether this is formalized as in submitting an article to a refereed journal or informal as in publishing a chapter in an edited book—and focused upon making a novel and self-contained contribution to the shared knowledge base of music therapy. Thus, the suggestions contained herein are directed primarily to professional books, monographs, chapters in edited books, various types of contributions to professional journals, contributions to online discussions, unpublished papers, conference proceedings, and presentations at conferences and symposia.

That much said, the contents of this publication are also applicable to other types of communications. Certainly much of the content can be directly applied to research reports, masters theses, doctoral dissertations, university lectures, and taking part in team meetings with other health care professionals. However, each of these communication forms has unique protocols and requirements, the elucidation of which goes beyond the scope of the present work. Thus, while I encourage you to make use of the information presented herein in formulating your contributions in these other formats, you may need to adapt some of the recommendations to the institutional requirements of the particular activity in which you are engaged.

There are three different types of professional communications discussed in this guide: theoretical and conceptual expositions, clinical case studies, and descriptions of forms of practice. This guide will not directly address considerations specific to research reports because they have many requirements and conventions that vary within different philosophical frameworks. However, researchers of all types will find that much of the content presented here is applicable to their writings, although some of the material will be more applicable in writing up qualitative research reports.

Along with the three *types* of communications, there are different *means* of communication as well: 1) providing information; 2) portraying the human reality of the music therapy process; and 3) presenting values, concepts, theories, and treatment frameworks, and relating them to clinical practice, education and training, and other professional issues. Of course, the content of any communication is information in a certain sense, but I have found it useful to maintain this tripartite division where the information category (1) is primarily concerned with conveying concrete techniques, interventions, strategies, and their associated treatment results. The portrayal of music therapy process (2) usually occurs through words, pictures, and/or sounds. The final category of presentation (3) necessarily has an abstract or conceptual component which may not be present in the other two categories.

The various types of communications make different uses of the different means for communicating. For example, in a case study there is a minimum of theory not to obscure the narrative flow, while in a theoretical exposition one includes clinical material sufficient to clarify the concepts being presented. Thus, being clear about the type of communication one is engaged in helps determine the relative balance of concepts, clinical examples, and concrete information to include.

## Theoretical and Conceptual Expositions

In creating professional communications of a theoretical nature it can be useful to understand which of the three types of theory listed below one is employing as it helps to determine the most suitable audience and supportive material to include. You can also take the opposite tack and choose the theoretical stance based on the primary audience you would like to reach.

### *Types of Theory*

The first type of communication to be discussed is one in which the goal is to put forward a conceptual, theoretical scheme or model, and possibly illustrate its connection to clinical practice. I have found it useful to conceptualize the type of theory being put forward in terms of its placement on a spectrum ranging from recontextualized theory where concepts are imported intact from related disciplines, to indigenous theory that is created primarily from experiences in music therapy. Within these two poles we find bridging theory that combines indigenous and imported constructs to varying degrees.[1]

Classifying theory in any domain is a complex undertaking that demands a comprehensive analysis and perspective—it is an essential scholarly endeavor in its own right. My intent in offering this schema is more pragmatic than it is scholarly. It is being put forward as an aid in planning communications, not as the result of fully researched and documented analysis. The boundaries between the types of theories are not rigid and the judgment as to where a particular theory lies on the spectrum is an individual one. It is important to identify the salient dimensions on which theories differ in order to determine how these differences influence the way we create professional communications.

*Recontextualized theory* seeks to describe and explain music therapy processes and phenomena in the terms of other disciplines such as psychoanalysis, neurology, or behavioral learning theory. Often these types of expositions are reductionistic because the constructs from other disciplines are presented as more fundamental than are those drawn from music therapy. Thus, music therapy phenomena are seen as being sufficiently explained when they can be completely rephrased or recontextualized in imported terms. In this type of theory the claim is often put forward that there should be a single foundational theory upon which all music therapy practices must be based. While I do not find the arguments for foundational

---

[1] Bruscia (1998a) describes the relationship of music therapy theory with other domains through the complementary processes of accommodation and assimilation: "In accommodation, phenomena in music therapy are fit into theories or constructs in other fields, and in the process, some aspect of music therapy is expanded, limited, revisioned, or modified to accommodate the other field. In assimilation, theories or constructs outside the field are modified to fit into music therapy. Here the external model is expanded, limited, revisioned or modified to accommodate music therapy phenomena" (p. 244). In addition, his concept of revisioned theory is similar to the idea of indigenous theory. Revisioned theory "consists of new conceptual schemes, propositions, and terminology, all created by the theorist to describe or explain music therapy phenomena in a way that breaks from past traditions, or takes them even further" (p. 245).

or recontextualized theory to be convincing, I refer the reader to Taylor (1997) for a well-developed, contemporary argument of this type.[2]

Here are examples of statements that reflect the use of recontextualized theory:

Music is an effective form of behavioral reinforcement.
Music allows for access to unconscious memories or repressed trauma.
Music is processed in the brain in a way that inhibits the transmission of pain signals.

*Recontextualized theory* has two primary purposes. It is useful if one's primary audience is outside of the music therapy profession because none of the concepts are specific to music therapy. There are no demands placed upon professionals from other domains to grapple with concepts or experiences which may be unfamiliar to them. Similarly, the use of recontextualized theory can serve to introduce music therapists to theory from other domains. Moreover, there may be pragmatic concerns for using this type of theory, such as the obtaining of funding for music therapy programs.

*Bridging theory* establishes connections between terms and concepts from different disciplines. Explanatory constructs from other areas are combined with those specific to music therapy. The external ideas can be used to form music- or music therapy-specific constructs and the purpose is to illuminate through analogy without making one discipline more fundamental than any other. Here are some examples:

First, consider the interest of the present author in new musicology concepts and what their application to music therapy can tell us about the connection between clinical and nonclinical music-making (Aigen, 2002). I have been exploring the concepts of vital drive and participatory discrepancies (Keil & Feld, 1994), which have been used in the analysis of interactions of jazz rhythm sections. I have noted that there are analogies between how a jazz rhythm section supports a soloist and how a music therapist

---

[2] Taylor would probably not agree that he is arguing for recontextualized theory, as he is critical of music therapy approaches that "define this discipline through its alignment with other intervention strategies that were not intended to include music" (1997, p. 4). However, in arguing for the necessity of a biomedical foundation for all music therapy practice he does seem to be placing the type of external constraint on music therapy theory that typifies recontextualized theory.

supports a client's expression. My belief is that studying the similarities and differences can enlighten us about both processes.

Another contemporary example is Pavlicevic (1997) who introduces the concept of dynamic form. She draws from philosophy (Susanne Langer in an indirect manner), and infant communication theory (Daniel Stern) in creating her concept, but notes that dynamic form is only present in clinical applications of music. In both examples, constructs are drawn from other disciplines which are then combined and applied in a unique way to illuminate music therapy process. However, there is no attempt to reframe music therapy processes completely within a construct borrowed from another domain, as one would do in recontextualized theory.

There are different reasons to employ bridging theory. As Pavlicevic (1997) discusses, different disciplines offer unique perspectives on music therapy phenomena. While each is potentially enriching, none of them fits music therapy in a neat way. The use of bridging theory recognizes this fact as it takes advantage of what other disciplines and other thinkers have to offer, while retaining the freedom to adapt and supplement the ideas with considerations unique to music therapy.

Bridging theories can be accessible to music therapists and to professionals and scholars from other disciplines. In terms of the latter, the use of language from other disciplines helps to establish a common area of discourse between music therapy and other professions. By supplementing the borrowed ideas with music therapy-specific constructs, one can contribute to the advancement of music therapy theory in a way that maintains its connections to other disciplines. I have also found that professionals and scholars from other domains usually respond positively to bridging theory. Having constructs from external domains applied to music therapy enlarges the domain of application of these constructs while simultaneously demonstrating the sophistication of music therapy practitioners and the unique contributions that music therapy can make to conceptions of music, human nature, and to the general understanding of cognitive and affective processes.

*Indigenous theory* is original and specific to music therapy. It is based on the idea that all disciplines begin by utilizing theory imported from other domains. As a particular area of human inquiry matures, its practitioners create and employ indigenous theory that is created primarily to explain the phenomena to which it is being applied. The underlying rationale is that all domains of inquiry have unique qualities and theory development proceeds in a direction that allows it to increasingly account for the unique issues in that domain. The Nordoff and Robbins (1977) concept of the music child is a good example of an indigenous construct. It is put forward as a means of explaining the originators' experiences with hundreds of disabled children over a period of many years. It is not a modification of a concept drawn from elsewhere, nor does it attempt to explain phenomena other than those that gave rise to it. Because of its highly specific nature, and because its saliency often depends upon a shared experiential base, indigenous theory is most appropriate when the primary audience is other music therapists and the purpose is to advance theoretical developments at the forefront of the profession.

### *Types of Theoretical Models*

Conceptual models can be developed for any of the three types of theory. I am using the term "model" here not as a synonym for an overall approach to music therapy, as Bruscia (1987a) does in the title of his text *Improvisational Models of Music Therapy.* Instead, I am using it in the more traditional way it is used in science as an iconic, structural, processual, or taxonomic representation of a process that illuminates aspects of the process through one of two ways: 1) establishing a similarity in structure between the model and the thing it represents; and 2) reducing a complex range of phenomena to a smaller number of basic concepts. An iconic model is an analogue of the thing it represents where the connection can be literal or metaphoric; the other types of models are classificatory and conceptual in nature and do not have a structural similarity with the phenomena being modeled. Examples of each of these types of models are offered below.

Models function in at least two ways: 1) to portray aspects of reality that underlie what is directly observed; and 2) to facilitate understanding by functioning as a heuristic device.[3] Theorists in music therapy have used a variety of kinds of models. Formulating an effective model is not just a way of presenting your ideas but is actually a way of developing them further

---

[3] Philosophers of science have traditionally disagreed over whether reality exists as portrayed in models (and theory in general) or whether theoretical entities are mere calculating or heuristic devices whose use leads to productive action. In the former perspective, Nordoff and Robbins's "music child" (Nordoff & Robbins, 1977) actually exists as a personality structure; in the latter way of thinking, this is just a useful metaphor which facilitates treatment and understanding.

because conceptual connections among phenomena can be revealed by the way that they are arranged in a model.

*Temporal models* are focused on time-based events. The two types are *stage models* and *process models*.

Stage models illustrate things such as sequential stages of the course of music therapy, the stages of an individual session, or the developmental stages of clients in music therapy. These models illustrate a sequential process where knowing the sequence of its elements facilitates understanding. In the text *Paths of Development in Nordoff-Robbins Music Therapy* (Aigen, 1998) I introduced two different stage models. The first one consisted of a model for the five stages of the music therapy session: Opening-Transition-Work-Transition-Closure. My research activities in that study of the Nordoff-Robbins clinical archives revealed an underlying aesthetic form in the sessions with one particular client. I suggested that knowing the form facilitated an understanding of the clinical-musical interventions, and that the stage of the session provided the necessary context for understanding the significance of the intervention. Thus, the qualities of each particular stage helped to explain why the therapist's music took the form that it did.

For example, in the case from which the model was derived, Paul Nordoff began the improvisations in some sessions with a consonant interval such as a fifth, while other sessions began with more dissonant intervals such as the tritone. These seemingly opposing musical strategies can be seen as reconciled when one understands the function of the opening stage, which is to establish a musical mood that can be developed in a variety of tonal and emotional directions as the client's needs dictate. Thus, the two types of openings differ in terms of their degree of dissonance, but they have in common the absence of strong sense of harmonic impetus in a specific direction. The opening tones provided an entry point that was free to be developed in a variety of directions. Considering the two seemingly opposing musical strategies in their function as part of the opening demonstrates their similarity on a more fundamental level of analysis. This reduction of a complexity of phenomena to a smaller number of conceptual categories is typical of all forms of systematic inquiry including scientific activity.

Another model in that text consisted of a four-stage model of the therapy process: Contact-Conflict-Consolidation-Closure. As I looked at musical interventions, e.g., choice of idiom and clinical strategies, e.g., confronting and challenging the client, I saw that both of these components of the therapists' activity changed radically over the course of therapy. Thus, if one wanted to understand when and how the original Nordoff-Robbins team would introduce songs, for example, or be more provocative in the musical interventions, one had to reference the stage of therapy the client was in. With both of these models, the purpose was to provide insight into the specifics of clinical interventions by showing them to be consequents of a more fundamental template.

Table 1.
Two Illustrations of a Temporal Model

| |
|---|
| *The Aesthetic Form of the Improvisational Music Therapy Session* |
| 1) Opening 2) Transition 3) Work 4) Transition 5) Closure |
| *Four-Stage Model of the Therapy Process* |
| 1) Contact 2) Conflict 3) Consolidation 4) Closure |

*Process models* illustrate an interactional process which occurs in time but where the particular sequence is not essential. An excellent example can be seen in Kenneth Bruscia's (1995a) study *Modes of Consciousness in Guided Imagery and Music*, the findings of which are displayed in Table 2. In that study he explores how the therapist expands, centers, and shifts consciousness in a GIM session. His analysis reveals four levels of experience: the sensory, affective, reflective, and intuitive; three types of worlds the therapist can occupy: the client's world, the personal world of the therapist, and the professional world of the therapist; five personal positions the therapist can take: fusion, accommodation, assimilation, differentiation, and objectification; and five media of transport: altered states of consciousness, music, imagery, physical interaction, and verbal interaction. Bruscia's explication of the experience of the GIM guide provides insight into the variety of means used in formulating and implementing clinical interventions.

Table 2.
Illustration of a Process Model

| |
|---|
| *Levels of Experience*<br>Sensory, Affective, Reflective, Intuitive |
| *Worlds to Occupy*<br>Client's, Therapist's Personal, Therapist's Professional |
| *Personal Positions*<br>Fusion, Accommodation, Assimilation, Differentiation, Objectification |
| *Media of Transport*<br>Altered States of Consciousness, Music, Imagery, Physical Interaction, Verbal Interaction |

Because it is time-based, a process model can develop into a stage model if it is discovered that the model's processes occur in a way that is sequentially meaningful. Thus, in some instances, the presentation of a stage model can represent further conceptual development on an existing process model. This is the case when we realize that the sequence of types of processes reveal a fundamental level of organization that was not immediately apparent.

For example, although an investigation of the sequence of the levels of experience, personal positions, and media of transport was beyond the scope of Bruscia's initial study, subsequent work (Bruscia, 1998b) revealed patterns in the sequencing of experience, positions, and media of transport that have led to further developments of the model that suggest it can be referenced to stages of the therapy process. Hence, it may eventually be fully presented as a stage model. In order to maintain the therapist's consciousness in the flexible and mobile state needed to effectively guide GIM sessions and to conduct improvisation sessions, a particular procedural cycle consisting of five phases was suggested: floating, checking in, shifting, reflection, and action. In this enhancement of the model, Bruscia has begun to reference particular levels of experience, and worlds to occupy, to particular places in the recommended procedural cycle. In exploring the various conditions under which the four aspects of the initial model present themselves an underlying template is created that can be of use in training those who lead GIM sessions.

*Taxonomic models* provide a descriptive overlay that brings organization to a domain through systematic classification. This type of classification is the basis for much of scientific knowledge such as that encoded in the periodic table of the elements, or in the classification of life through the various categories of species, genus, family, etc. This type of classification is essential to the theoretical advancement of any domain of inquiry because it reduces the fantastic diversity of the natural world to a more manageable number of categories. Considering the way in which the world is ordered is one of the prime ways scientists are stimulated to create theory. Darwin's theory of evolution would be inconceivable without the systematic categorization of life produced by his precursors such as Linnaeus.

At times, the structure of a taxonomic model reflects aspects of the phenomena it is representing and at times its structure is more arbitrary. Consider Nordoff and Robbins's (1971) model of the musical responses of disabled children in improvisational music therapy:

Table 3.
Illustration of a Taxonomic Model

| *Categories of Response* |
|---|
| 1. Complete Rhythmic Freedom |
| 2. Unstable Rhythmic Freedom |
| 3. Limited Rhythmic Freedom |
| 4. Compulsive Beating |
| 5. Disordered Beating |
| 6. Evasive Beating |
| 7. Emotional-Force Beating |
| 8. Chaotic-Creative Beating |
| 9. Piano Playing |
| 10. Responses by Singing |
| 11. Responses to Singing |
| 12. Responses to Specific Musical Idioms |
| 13. Responses to Mood or Changes of Mood in Music |

In general, the sequence of the categories in this taxonomy does not appear to reflect any type of hierarchy or developmental process, although the names of the first three categories give some indication that there are more clinically desirable states for the clients to be in as they represent a greater flexibility in musical expression than some of the other states. But at times we create taxonomic models in which the ordering of its elements does reflect an essential aspect of the domain it is representing. Consider the following model (Aigen, 1995a, p. 25) that is based upon a hierarchical relationship among its components:

Table 4.
Illustration of a Taxonomic Model Structured Conceptually

| *Four Levels of Interaction With/In Music* | |
|---|---|
| LEVEL 4 | Affective Musical Expression |
| LEVEL 3 | Aesthetic Musical Awareness/Creation |
| LEVEL 2 | Dynamic Musical Intelligence |
| LEVEL 1 | Concrete/Basic Musical Skills |

This was a model proposed to account for the wide range of clinical activities and focuses that characterize contemporary Nordoff-Robbins practice. The model is hierarchical in the sense that skills on the higher levels (toward 4) presuppose the existence of skills on the lower levels (toward 1). Thus, its structure—that is, the sequence of levels—is not arbitrary but reflects the domain it is representing.

In presenting a model such as this, it can very helpful to present concrete examples of the conceptual categories. So in the publication in which this model first appears (Aigen, 1995a, p. 30), after presenting the conceptual model, I presented an illustration of the model in terms of melody:

Table 5.
Illustration of a Taxonomic Model with Examples

| *Illustration of the Model in Terms of Melody* | |
|---|---|
| LEVEL 4 | Infusing/recognizing aspects of one's emotions in a melody |
| LEVEL 3 | Creating or hearing the interesting or novel aspect of a melody |
| LEVEL 2 | Hearing why a melody is constructed as it is |
| LEVEL 1 | Understanding that a melody exists |

The last step in the development of this particular model was to add a horizontal dimension for complexity. In this study I focused more on providing an overview of practice for a particular treatment model than on looking at client development. So I was careful to say that client development was not necessarily modeled by progress through this model.

Two of the most comprehensive taxonomies in the music therapy literature are the "Improvisation Assessment Profiles" (IAPs) and "Sixty-Four Clinical Techniques in Improvisational Music Therapy," both of which are from Bruscia (1987a). The IAPs provide a system of analyzing client improvisations in music therapy according to six profiles: integration, variability, tension, congruence, salience, and autonomy. Each profile has a similar five-level gradient along which the improvisations are analyzed.

Although the IAPs are currently the object of renewed interest, I would like to direct the reader's attention to the clinical techniques for the purposes of the present discussion. The techniques are presented within nine subgroups according to their primary clinical function. In discussing them, Bruscia highlights some of the challenges in creating a taxonomy, such as resolving the confusion of terminology when the different practitioners from whose work the techniques emerged used similar terms in different ways and different terms to mean the same thing. The chapter in which the techniques are presented (Bruscia, 1987a, pp. 535–537) is especially recommended as it is a paradigmatic example of how to present a taxonomy within its clinical context along with an acknowledgment of the methodological problems and solutions in creating and presenting the taxonomy.

Table 6.
Illustration of a Taxonomic Model Structured Functionally

| *Sixty-Four Clinical Techniques in Improvisational Music Therapy* | |
|---|---|
| Techniques of Empathy | Emotional Exploration Techniques |
| Structuring Techniques | Referential Techniques |
| Techniques of Intimacy | Discussion Techniques |
| Elicitation Techniques | Redirection Techniques |
| Procedural Techniques | |

*Integrating Clinical Examples in Theoretical Expositions*

Successful theory communications make effective but judicious use of clinical examples. Whereas the primary purpose of clinical examples in case study presentations is to present the living reality of music therapy work, in theory communications the purpose is to illustrate the theory, make it more comprehensible, and demonstrate the utility of the theory by grounding it in practice. The clinical examples can be drawn from many individuals if so desired, and in fact, this is a strength as it can demonstrate the breadth of the application of the theory.

In constructing explanations of the clinical material it is normally not so important to have a chronologically structured narrative, unless the theory being presented is in the form of a developmental or stage model. If there is a temporal component to the model, the illustrations can be comprised of many individuals at different stages or one individual at various stages. Most important, demonstrating how a theory is grounded in clinical practice enhances the ability of others to generalize from it. In this regard, utilizing a variety of individuals in an illustrative way increases the likelihood that the audience/readers will perceive similarities between the clients presented and their own clients, again enhancing their ability to apply the theory.

In general, complex theory is more suitable for publications than for live presentations because of the opportunity readers have to study and assimilate the material at an individual pace. Presentations are useful venues to sketch out the general ideas behind a theory and they serve to point people to writings, whether these are published or unpublished manuscripts. And presentations offer the opportunity to illustrate theory with audiovisual presentations of clinical material not typically available in publications. So if you are presenting theory, whenever possible take advantage of these opportunities.

**Clinical Case Studies**

Before going into detail about the considerations involved in creating effective case studies, it is important to first mention that it is essential to obtain the permission of clients or their guardians before revealing confidential information in any professional forum. The code of ethics of the American Music Therapy Association (AMTA, 2001) has two clauses that bear on this issue. Clause 3.12.2c of the code says that confidential information may only be released with client consent. And clause 3.12.4 asserts that client identity must be disguised when case materials are used for research and teaching. While publications and professional presentations are not mentioned specifically, it can be assumed that these forums are covered by the teaching and research clause. However, there are circumstances that affect how these clauses are interpreted and implemented—such as when a child's name is sung in a song, or videotape recordings are used for research, teaching, and the dissemination of information—and it is essential to get explicit permission from clients and guardians for each particular use of confidential case material.

In this section, I will discuss the presentation of a case study where the primary focus is providing the story of an individual or group because of its compelling aspects or inherent human drama. That is, case studies can be used for a variety of other purposes—such as illustrating a theory, exemplifying a particular clinical approach, or demonstrating a domain of practice—but I would like to make some comments on the presentation of case studies where the focus is conveying the meaning of a significant clinical process.

Case studies are possibly the most important form of professional publication for music therapy clinicians: they educate and inspire us; they can reveal potentials in the work that we may not have considered; and they are a way of establishing connections with other professionals across large expanses of culture, geography, and time, in a manner that supports us through what can be lonely work. And because the presentational form of case study approximates the natural forms of reporting engaged in by clinicians as part of their daily activities, case studies are well suited to conveying information that can be applied to other clients.

The case study format is congruent with the needs of the working clinician because it is "epistemologically in harmony with the [clinician's] experience and thus to that person a natural basis for generalization" (Stake, 1978, p. 5). Because the realm of application for clinicians is the particular individual, case studies provide essential information that is impossible to convey through other types of reports that either deal with classes or types of people, or that do not provide enough detail for clinicians to apply the information conveyed to the individuals with whom they work.

The reporting of case studies require strong narrative structure and flow, typically a chronological one, in which the aesthetic dimensions of the communication become relatively more important than is the case in a predominantly theoretical exposition. This makes it engaging for an audience and reflects the importance of myth and story in human understanding. Story is an important means for the presentation and assimilation of information and at times the importance of "making a good story" is minimized in professional communications because it is felt that the agenda of professional communications is to increase understanding and aesthetic considerations regarding narrative structure are not relevant to this task.

I would like to briefly take issue with this conception and thereby provide a firmer foundation for the presence of stronger narratives in our professional communications. First, the delivery of information does not exhaust all of the possible purposes of professional communication. We want to convey the human realities of our clients in music therapy and we want to also inspire our colleagues through these stories. This is an important component of some professional communications, one which especially relies on strong narrative elements.

Second, even a nonexperiential, conceptual presentation benefits from attention paid to aesthetic considerations. For example, the symmetry, balance, and elegance of a model aids in its comprehension. Aesthetic factors are not frills added on to human experience but are essential components of this experience and their presence facilitates the acquisition of many kinds of knowledge.

Last, when our focus is to create a vicarious experience in our audience, to have them experience in a vital way some of what we have experienced as music therapists, it is essential to pay attention to the aesthetic factors which draw in audience members to the experience. This type of presentation makes a greater impression on the mind of the listener/reader as it is brought more into the person's core. Remember, the individuals are not present to illustrate a process, technique, or approach but because of the inherent meaning of the experience. Thus, there is an obligation on the part of the author/presenter to provide comprehensiveness rather than a selective or narrow focus.

This is facilitated by including the client's perspective if possible. Numerous examples of the client's perspective on music therapy can be found in Hibben (1999) and examples of published case studies of the type being discussed here are Stephens (1981) and Aigen (1990). Gillian Stephens's introduction to her case study on Adele elegantly explains her purpose in its writing while simultaneously creating the appropriate mood and state of mind for reading the article. The rhythm and meaning of her words prepare us to read in a different way from how we typically approach professional publications:

Example 1.
Introduction to a Case Study

---

This is the story of Adele.

Adele gave me the opportunity to examine my work in a very special way. All my work was as if done for the first time. I could take nothing for granted. I had to dig deep into myself to understand what I was seeing, to discover how I could make decisions, and how, as a music therapist, I could begin to work.

I wish to share this process, this struggle, and, through the silence . . . Adele. (Stephens, 1981, p. 25)

When we discuss clients with the intention of illustrating a particular theory or model, the organization of the communication typically follows the structure of the theory or model being illustrated. Usually, the stance that the author/presenter takes is a detached one appropriate to the subject matter. When we discuss a client because of some fundamental human concerns and qualities exemplified by the client and the clinical process, there are other types of choices one can make.

First, it is important to consciously decide the degree to which your own subjective experience will be part of the communication. Sometimes, it is effective to function as the author/narrator of a clinical story without revealing too much of one's inner process as a therapist because to do so might deflect attention from the real object of interest, the client's story. At other times, it can be quite enlightening for both professional and lay audiences to hear about the therapist's inner process as the client's story unfolds. Some might go as far to say that any significant therapy process is always the story of how therapist and client(s) mutually affect one another and any story that omits the therapist's process is incomplete.

The choice you make on this matter should reflect the content of the story being told. Is the story primarily one where a client showed significant growth, evidenced capacities not available outside the music therapy session, or revealed something profound about universal human concerns? If so, then as the storyteller you may want to take a more transparent role and allow the client's process to speak for itself. On the other hand, if the story is primarily one that challenged you as a therapist, gave you new insights into the nature of music therapy process, or was one in which you were profoundly influenced by the therapy process, then it would be warranted to include a significant amount of content on your own impressions, reactions, and on the impact of the process on your own life, professional and otherwise. However, it is essential to ensure that the content on you as a therapist is in service of the overall goal of enlightening the audience about the various dimensions of music therapy practice rather than meeting your own need for self-revelation, something that is a danger whenever we make ourselves the object of our professional communications.

Second, it is also important to consider the type of language you will use in telling a clinical story. When the focus is on conveying the nature of music therapy in a direct and unmediated fashion, it is generally recommended that theoretical, medical, and professional terms be avoided as much as possible. The use of such terms tends to distance the reader from the emotional immediacy of the experience. In other words, if as the author/presenter you assume a more distanced stance as indicated by the choice of language that is more distant from direct experience, you cannot expect your audience to be involved on an emotional level in the story you are telling.

This does not mean that you must avoid theoretical constructs entirely in such a case study, but instead the conceptual material must be provided in a way that it enhances the clinical narrative rather than distracting from it, much in the way it was recommend that the therapist's personal material be integrated. An excellent example of a case study reported in this fashion is in Colin Lee's (1996) book *Music at the Edge: The Music Therapy Experiences of a Musician with AIDS.* Consider Lee's description of his text:

Example 2.
Introduction to a Case Study

---

This book describes an extraordinary flight in music therapy with Francis, a musician who lived with and died of AIDS. It will trace the re-awakening of his creative musical spirit. . . . Francis and I explored many regions as client and therapist during the last year of his life; this story is a testament to his journey towards death. . . . I will also describe my involvement in the therapy process: my searchings and reflections, and the professional personal challenges this extraordinary experience of "therapy in music" brought into my life.

> The book is essentially non-academic: all theoretical constructs . . . appear naturally as the text unfolds. The reader, uninitiated in this area of practice, whether layman, musician, health care professional or student, will be able to comprehend the content fully, with little or no previous knowledge of music therapy. (p. 1)

Note how Lee prepares his audience by describing the rationale for the level of candor and self-revelation in which he subsequently engages, and for the offering of some conceptual material whose purpose is to enrich the chronological telling of this particular clinical story.

A final area to consider in writing a case study is probably the most important one and the most difficult one to address. This concerns how to decide which material to include and how to prepare it for publication. Most case studies are prepared for dissemination after the therapy process has concluded. This means that they are created from session notes and, in some cases, audio or video recordings of the therapy sessions. In either case, usually there is more material to draw from than can be included in a case study report and the author's/presenter's primary task is one of winnowing and selecting clinical material.

Although I believe that aesthetic concerns are prominent on many levels of music therapy process, courses of therapy are not themselves aesthetic objects. Thus, fashioning a strong narrative from the raw session material means either drawing from the material an underlying structure that may only be implicit in the actual events of the therapy process, or imposing a structure upon the process from without. And to some degree, it is a matter of judgment to determine which strategy more accurately characterizes a given case study. But in both cases, there are interpretive choices made by the author[4] that are necessary to create a coherent narrative. Good writing demands that we make such choices and scholarly standards demand that we provide to our audience the criteria that guide our choices. Hence, just because a process of therapy proceeded in fits and starts, contained unforeseen interruptions, and may not have concluded in a satisfactory fashion, does not mean that our report of such a process cannot itself be expressed through a product that is complete, coherent, and ultimately satisfying to the reader. We may want to portray experiences of a splintered or dissociated

---

[4] I am using the term "author" here to indicate either a writer or a presenter of a case study.

experience of life, but this does not mean that our expression of such experiences is itself splintered or lacking unity and organization.

In choosing which events to include in a case study, there are a few different considerations to keep in mind. First, think about the most moving, powerful, or profound moments in the process, both for your client as well as yourself, depending upon the stance you are taking regarding the role of your self-revelation. Certainly, many of these moments are central to the reason you are reporting this particular case study and is logical to include them in your report. Second, you should also include what may be considered turning points in the process. In what sessions did you first perceive the inception of a new development on the client's part? When did you first see or hear the client move past internal or external barriers to achieve a more gratifying experience? When did the client first exhibit a new way of relating or self-expression? All of these moments provide important nodal points whose explication helps to create a skeletal structure upon which a successful case study report depends.

Also, do not minimize the importance of including material that serves primarily to illustrate typical sessions and interactions, regardless of whether there was anything exceptional of note in that session. That which is extraordinary can appear to be more so when reported against the background of the more mundane. And sometimes the most important aspects of the process from the client's perspective are built more from the steady support, reassurance, and security provided in everyday, ongoing clinical interactions than from those moments that the therapist might identify as being more profound, powerful, or unique.

If you are unsure about how to structure the case study one option is first assemble all of the profound, nodal, and exemplary interactions that you would like to include, identify the various themes that relate them to one another, and write the study around the clinical examples that you have selected. Here, for the most part, the selection of case material precedes the articulation of a thematic structure. Of course, there will always be an interaction between the form of the report and the excerpts selected, however it is possible to put greater emphasis on beginning from the interactions and developing the form around them.

In structuring a case study, a tension can arise between the conflicting needs of accurately charting the developmental processes of the client and addressing topics of general significance and application. One way of resolving this tension is to structure a case study around the basic issues or themes of the therapy process. Some clients work in different areas in therapy, and while they are all related in some way, they can represent relatively discrete clinical focuses. In these cases, you may want to organize the report by clinical theme or issue and then follow a chronological development within the sections devoted to each theme.

In a recent publication (Aigen, 2002), I reported on a seven-and-a-half-year course of therapy with a client named Lloyd that I engaged in jointly with a fellow therapist, Alan Turry. With such a long treatment process, there were a number of ways to structure the report and in the publication I included some thoughts on this in order to facilitate the reader's understanding of the study's structure. I did this because I felt it would enhance the reader's comprehension to know why the material was ordered in the way that it was. Here is how this was described:

Example 3.
Introduction to a Case Study Explaining Its Structure

---

While Lloyd has worked on many areas simultaneously throughout his course of therapy—including the motoric, the cognitive, the expressive, the aesthetic, and the relational—it is nonetheless possible to discern three broad themes which sequentially characterized different (but overlapping) stages of his course of therapy. It is the nature of these three themes which form the structure of this monograph .The first goal area for Lloyd was developing the ability to sustain musical participation, and once established, to differentiate this participation through various stylistic structures. . . . The second goal area . . . involved developing a greater degree of musical closeness with the therapists which was accompanied by a significantly enhanced ability to participate in music of increasingly greater expressive variation and affective content. . . . The third and final area of focus took place solely through Lloyd's work at the piano. . . . He began by recapitulating some of the work on the other two instruments, developing stability in his playing. . . . He became able to develop this stability into a more differentiated forms of expression, playing the piano with ever-developing skill and grace in an ever-widening variety of musical moods. The three chapters that follow are patterned after these three main streams of clinical development. Within each stream, different techniques, observations and themes are highlighted as they became more prominent in Lloyd's therapy process. (Aigen, 2002, pp. 28–29)

With this explanation in hand, the reader is prepared for an account that is divided into three theme areas and that is presented chronologically within each area. Because the three areas overlap somewhat, there is a general chronological presentation which accounts for the sequence in which the three themes are presented.

Although Chapter 3 of the present text addresses some differences between writing and presenting, there are a few aspects of this issue relevant specifically to the type of case study we are discussing. First, presenters have the option to include audio and video recordings in order to make the presentation come alive. Although there is this possibility in publications, in general the inclusion of different type of media is more problematic in conjunction with a publication. This means that the clinical component must be able to be captured verbally. In a presentation, including a strong theoretical component is not as essential as in a publication where the inclusion of conceptual and theoretical material often serve as the rationale for the publication. And complex theory is more easily assimilated in a publication where the reader can stop, reflect on the material, and reread material that is particularly difficult. Presenting complex theory in a conference presentation does not afford the audience the luxury of taking in the material at an individualized pace. So in determining the most suitable venue for a case study you should answer the following questions: 1) Is the case study primarily valuable because of its inherent human and clinical interest, or is its primary value in illustrating a theory or model of practice? 2) Can the clinical component be adequately conveyed verbally or is this dependent upon supportive media? The answers to these questions can help you decide the best type of venue for presenting the case study.

## Forms of Clinical Practice

Some music therapists may want to share aspects of how they implement music therapy with their clients but are uncertain about how to frame the knowledge that they would like to pass on. It is very important to be able to formulate the focus of our communication, whether this is a model of practice, a particular procedure, a clinical technique, a domain of application, or a topic of general interest across various treatment domains. First, we can not expect our audience to come away with a clear message unless our communication contains one. Also, the main body of our communication always needs supportive material to frame it (presentationally) and contextualize it (conceptually). The choice of the correct framing material stems from how we conceive our central message. When we want to communicate aspects of our clinical approach, there are various ways to conceive of the central focus. Here are different types of focuses, each with an accompanying example:

Table 7.
Types of Focus with Examples

| Type of Focus | Example |
| --- | --- |
| A model of practice | *Guided Imagery and Music in Group Settings* |
| A music therapy procedure | *Songwriting with Adolescents* |
| A clinical technique | *Musical Reflections of Nonverbal Behavior* |
| A domain of application | *Musically-Assisted Childbirth* |
| A topic of general interest across treatment domains | *The Relationship Between Lyrics and Musical Structures in Song in Music Therapy* |

These different categories are not necessarily mutually exclusive and one communication could fit into different categories. Yet it is still helpful to determine the primary purpose behind one's communication and structure it accordingly.

In these various types of presentations, clinical examples serve the secondary purpose of illustrating principles, methods, or techniques. Thus, a case may be used to illustrate the primary topic, but these communications are not case studies per se. One of the differences is that in a clinical case study we generally want to chronologically present a comprehensive portrait of the clinical work. In the types of presentations listed above a certain selectivity or narrowness of focus is often warranted and a chronological approach is not always essential or appropriate.

Let us examine the various examples in Table 7 in terms of the appropriate material to include given the nature of each focus. These are not intended as exhaustive recommendations but are instead offered to suggest the type of thinking one should engage in while planning communications that focus upon forms of practice.

First is the hypothetical *Guided Imagery and Music in Group Settings.* What type of supportive material should be included in such a communication? If the focus is on GIM as a model of practice it is clear that it would be more appropriate to include material on the model and contextualize the communication within the practice of GIM than it would be to include significant amounts of material on typical practices in group music therapy. If part of the interest of such a topic is exploring how a model frequently implemented with individuals is done with groups, then it would be better to describe the aspects of the model that are common and that vary in both realms of application. Of course, one could make the opposite choice and situate the practice of GIM in group settings in relation to other group music therapy approaches; however, this would involve a shift of the focus from the model (GIM) to a domain of application (group music therapy.)

Similarly, in the communication *Songwriting with Adolescents* the focus is on a particular procedure. Again, the related and supportive material should frame and contextualize the procedure rather than the domain of application, if it is the procedure that is of greatest interest. So in this instance it might be recommended to include material such as alternative uses of songs in music therapy—for example, as a vehicle to stimulate discussion, and the process of improvising songs as opposed to composing them. The supportive material serves to put the audience's attention where the author/presenter wants it, on the procedure of songwriting. Developing a consistency of focus among the primary and supportive materials will make the final product function better as a teaching tool, which is the primary purpose behind creating it.

In the focus on technique embodied in *Musical Reflections of Nonverbal Behavior* different considerations would come into play. Other types of therapists take nonverbal expressions into account: dance-movement therapists work directly with them and verbal psychotherapists can choose to focus and comment upon them. What might be of greatest interest in this type of communication are the unique possibilities that arise when music is brought into the situation. Thus, it might be more interesting to contextualize this communication in relation to other ways of responding therapeutically to nonverbal behavior rather than in relation to musical reflections of verbal expressions.

When we consider a domain of application, such as *Musically-Assisted Childbirth*, we usually want to contextualize the communication within typical problems and interventions in the domain. In other words, there are many areas of human functioning in which music is used as an assistive tool, such as in cognitive learning and gait rehabilitation. These would not typically be of interest to the reader who is drawn in by the focus on childbirth, however. What would be of interest are the various needs of women in childbirth, such as distraction and pain relief, and the variety of tools used to accomplish these aims, such as breathing techniques and medications. This would be the supportive material that would best highlight the unique contribution of music therapy in this domain, and would probably take precedence over summarizing existing practices in medical music therapy as another option.

There is greater flexibility in framing a topic of general interest that is relevant in a variety of models and domains of application such as is embodied in the topic *The Relationship Between Lyrics and Musical Structures in Song in Music Therapy*. Such a topic is of potential relevance to the largest number of music therapists because it is not limited in terms of the age, clinical need, or functioning level of the client, nor is it specific to a particular model of treatment.

There are at least two ways to approach such a topic in deciding upon the supportive and contextual material. First, it is possible to take a creative approach and look at the topic as one that addresses the two tools of music and words in music therapy. Seen this way, it would be possible to discuss other investigations of the varying uses of words and music, even though these other publications may not have been discussing songs. Second, it would be interesting as well to go outside the domain of music therapy to include material on the way that music is used in popular or classical song to enhance or comment upon the meaning behind song lyrics.

In sum, although there is no specific formula for determining how best to contextualize forms of practice, the most important guideline is to choose the material that enhances the audience's understanding of your central message.

CHAPTER 2

# Common Areas of Concern for Writing and Presenting

## Agendas and Motivations

As was mentioned previously, there is no such thing as not having an agenda in our communications, although at times we may not be fully cognizant of our motivations in this regard. Nevertheless, our obligation is to be fully aware of our own agendas, and inform our professional audiences whenever this is appropriate. The honesty of acknowledging that there is a rhetorical or persuasive element in professional communications allows us the freedom to engage in it. Here is an example I included at the conclusion of a chapter introducing the principles of qualitative research:

Example 4. Acknowledging One's Writing Agenda

---

I admit to having an agenda in writing this chapter. That agenda is to convince you, the reader, of the intellectual rigor of qualitative research as well as the value of this approach for music therapy. In addition, I acknowledge that I possess a certain conception of qualitative research that is not universally subscribed to, either in the profession of music therapy or in the larger sphere of academia. My hope has been that by being forthcoming about these personal preferences, I have given you important information in judging what I have written as well as demonstrated the value of disclosing such information. All writers have agendas, whether they are acknowledged or not. Such acknowledgment does not make us any less scholarly, scientific, or responsible, but more so. (Aigen, 1995b, p. 309)

Writers, presenters, and their audiences want the same thing. This is to exchange information and experiences at the heart of their practice. We all want to communicate those things which are most important to us as music therapists. Our challenge is to allow our scholarly and academic standards to flexibly evolve to accommodate these needs while articulating new evaluation standards appropriate to new forms of interaction.

There are many different motivations that we possess for wanting to share information with colleagues. While they are not mutually exclusive, it is nonetheless important to discern your motivation in order to be in a position to best fashion and deliver your message:

*Clarify One's Own Thinking.* In my professional and academic work I have often heard people say that they have a "writing problem." The implication was that they had thoughts and concepts that they had difficulty putting on paper. Yet, more often than not, the writing problem was really a thinking problem. That is, the difficulty was more of conceptualization than it was of the mechanical operation of putting thoughts fully fleshed out into a written form. I have found that the process of putting together a presentation or publication is an excellent vehicle for organizing and stimulating my own thinking. It is not as if I often have a fully fleshed out conceptual scheme prior to preparing the professional communication and the writing part is a mere recording of ideas already thought. The process of preparing communications is simultaneously a process of developing one's thinking in a given area.

*Gain Professional Esteem and Recognition.* It is a legitimate professional need to be recognized by one's peers, something present in all areas of human endeavor. Professional activities in music therapy rarely bring any kind of tangible benefit other than the intrinsic reward of doing quality work in one's area of expertise. Gaining the respect and esteem of our colleagues is one of the few benefits that we can obtain from the many hours of work spent preparing professional communications.

Because there are so few tangible or material benefits from the time we spend in preparing communications it is essential that we learn to provide recognition to each other. It has been my experience that most authors of music therapy works—ranging from those who have written articles in lesser known journals to authors of well-known books—feel that colleagues rarely take the time to engage them about their writings. Too often, authors feel as if their work, once published, disappears into a void. The desire for professional recognition is a healthy one which can serve as an important motivator to elevate the profession of music therapy by encouraging professionals to share their work and ideas.

*Influence the Evolution of the Profession and Discipline.*[1] Because I believe in the advocacy model of professional activity, I recognize that our communications are oriented toward having an effect upon the profession. Personally, I want to have this effect. I want to embody and promote the values which I believe will enhance clinical training and the experiences of clients in music therapy. This may not be a legitimate motivation in the neutrality model of professional relationships. However, if one accepts that values guide all of our interactions, both within our professional activities and outside them, then we ought to do this in an overt way rather than in a less than fully conscious way.

*Educate Colleagues.* It is important to recognize that we possess skills, information, and ways of thinking that our colleagues can benefit from. Certainly it is false modesty to pretend otherwise. In fact, if we believe that we possess information, skills, and ways of thinking that would benefit their work, we have an ethical obligation to provide these things to our colleagues. The desire to educate others demonstrates our obligation to our professional community, and by extension, to the many clients seen by our colleagues.

*Share Experience.* In our clinical work, we may have musical and interpersonal experiences that are unique, novel, or profound. We witness people both at their most vulnerable and at their most capable and courageous moments. It is human nature to want to share the nature of our experience with others who can understand what we have experienced. The act of preparing for and engaging in the communication of our experience helps us to validate the nature of our experience and to assimilate it into our private and professional selves.

*Meet Extrinsic Requirements.* Too often we consider professional requirements placed on us by employers and certification bodies as a burden rather than as an opportunity. Academic colleagues complain about the requirement to "publish or perish" and music therapy clinicians can feel that the need to impress employers through presentations or publications is burdensome. Yet, we can turn these necessities to our favor and actually appreciate that employers require activities that benefit us professionally and

---

[1] Throughout this paper I refer to the "profession and discipline" of music therapy using Bruscia's (1987b) important distinction between the profession, the realm of activity involving relationships among music therapists, and the discipline, the realm of activity involving relationships between music therapists and their clients.

bring a service to our colleagues as well. The fact is, many music therapists may be engaged in professional communications of one kind or another not because they want to, but because of demands placed on them by others. However, once you are able to find ways to frame your most pressing concerns and interests within a professional communication, your feelings about these activities, initially undertaken for extrinsic reasons, can transform as they become activities with intrinsic gratification.

*Enhance the Quality of Service to Clients.* Although this comes last in this brief list, it is actually the most important consideration. Music therapy is a service profession; our work exists to enhance the lives of others. In fact, this consideration underlies all the others. If we cannot articulate how a particular communication will benefit clients, directly or indirectly, then I suggest that the content of the communication needs to be reevaluated.

Of course there are probably other types of motivations not listed here and I encourage you to become aware of your own. Doing so will help you decide what material to include in your communication and how to frame it. Understanding your own motivation also helps you decide how much personal information to include. My own guideline is that we provide that level of personal information which is necessary for the audience or reader to best understand our message. Thus, the personal information is never present for its own sake or to meet our need for self-revelation; on the other hand, we have license to include that information which best serves our message.

## Differentiating Between a Topic and a Focus

This discussion of the motivating factors behind our communication leads us into examining the difference between a topic and a focus. The topic is the subject of the article or presentation. This can be a particular client, therapy group, method, approach, or professional issue, for example. The topic logically precedes the focus and is often the first thing you settle on. The nature of the topic usually stays constant throughout your preparations.

In contrast, the focus is the particular aspect of the topic you are presenting, or a particular perspective on the topic. The focus can evolve as you put the work together and any one topic can yield a wide variety of focuses. Occasionally our focus precedes the articulation of a topic, but this can cause difficulty in organization as we present material without a clear rationale for why it is included and we have difficulties in deciding what material to include, how to frame it, and how to sequence it.

For example, consider a research study that I engaged in which, when presented publicly, comprised three different focuses. These different focuses led to different publications and presentations and the fact that it was a research study is not important to illustrate the difference between a topic and focus. The topic was one year in an adolescent music therapy group. Once I spent the year observing the group I knew that I wanted to communicate different aspects of the group through different means.

The first communication I developed was a conference presentation where the particular focus was illustrating the process of a clinical qualitative research study conducted in line with the principles of Naturalistic Inquiry *(Focus One)*. So while I did present aspects of the clinical work and group process, these were contextualized in a way that illustrated how the different procedures of qualitative research were implemented and how the findings of the study reflected the particular form of inquiry chosen. Second, I wrote a research monograph (Aigen, 1997) that focused on how the stages of the group process reflected those drawn from group therapy theory *(Focus Two)*. Last, I put together a training video entitled "Improvised Song in Group Music Therapy" whose focus was the way in which the improvised song lyrics of the group members reflected the stages of the group's development *(Focus Three)*. So these three particular professional communications shared one topic (the actual therapy process of the group studied) while representing three quite different focuses. The focuses varied according to the suitability of each medium for presenting different kinds of information and experiences and the specific nature of each focus meant that very different supportive and contextualizing material was included in each communication.

## Developing a Topic

Almost any topic can be the subject of scholarly, professional inquiry if it is approached systematically, with a seriousness of purpose, and it is relevant to the activities of music therapists. Professional and scholarly standards for publications and presentations evolve in response to a changing world with interests and values that are constantly being reshaped in response to human needs. You can play a role in this evolution through your choice of topics for communication. Our professional communications define our professional domain, and by being present in them you are helping to define the practice itself and the types of considerations that are relevant in this work.

In 1991 I published an article (Aigen, 1990) entitled "Echoes of Silence" in the journal *Music Therapy*. In it, I wanted to focus on a number of areas which I felt were important but which seemed to be scarce in the professional literature in music therapy. Some of these elements included the therapist's subjective experience, the nature of the real relationship to the client, and a portrait of the clinical process with a client who demonstrated strength and fortitude in the face of debilitating fears. But I wanted to present them without interpretation or the filter of a theory which I believed would distance the reader from the experience that I hoped to create. I deliberately wanted to find a responsible way to bring these elements into a professional, juried journal such as *Music Therapy* in order to have an impact on what was considered appropriate writings for professional publications.

I was somewhat humbled a few years later when I realized how much of the content and tone of my article was influenced by the article of Gillian Stephens (1981) referred to previously. The two articles shared a similarity in title, in client profile, and even in the way the clinical work was described. However, there were some elements in my publication which were not in Stephens's, primarily pertaining to the relevance of this type of clinical report in the context of qualitative research and the building of indigenous theory in music therapy, both of which were very scarce in the music therapy literature in 1981 but were beginning to be more overtly discussed in 1991. Gillian Stephens's pioneering article paved the way for my own and in fact, made it possible.

This is how our professional communications can create a dialogue with each other, a dialogue of ideas, values, and concepts which can transcend the individuals involved. Our communications continue to echo within everyone who comes into contact with them and it is incumbent upon us to make the best use of the platforms afforded to us by our colleagues to promote client welfare.

So in developing a topic, I suggest that you begin with what is most meaningful, compelling, interesting, stimulating, and relevant to you and to your work. Why communicate anything that does not have these qualities? Doing so provides you with the motivation to sustain long and difficult labors. Moreover, when a topic is compelling to you it is possible to make it compelling to your audience.

There are a number of places to begin in developing a topic:

*A Profound Experience with a Client or Group.* At times we are moved by our clients and the courage, strength, and fortitude that they show. Such experiences have inherent human value and also tend to be exemplary illustrations of music therapy process. Think of clients who made notable progress, whose humanity touched you as they demonstrated admirable human qualities such as courage or a generosity of spirit. Or perhaps you have worked with clients who functioned radically different in music and music therapy from how they functioned in other areas, or whose musical expression was particularly profound. All of these experiences can form the foundation for professional communications that can have a positive impact on our profession.

*A Way of Working You Have Expertise In.* Some music therapists develop the desire to present and write about their work primarily because they have developed an advanced, specialized set of skills. This can be conceptualized through any of the forms referred to in Table 7 on page 22. These can include a particular procedure such as songwriting, a particular realm of application such as music therapy with expectant mothers, or any other specialized domain of application.

*A Novel Way of Thinking About Music Therapy.* One way that our profession develops is through shifts in consciousness about what we consider the essence of music therapy practice to be. Very often we are greatly influenced by ideas, concepts, and theories from other realms of human inquiry. Illustrating the value of a body of literature that you have found particularly useful in developing music therapy applications is an excellent basis for a presentation or article. An example would include applying the tenets of family therapy, or any group therapy model, to music therapy. Related to the new application of related literature bases to music therapy would be a novel application for a particular setting, such as "Music Psychotherapy in a Rehabilitation Setting." All of our professional communications should be advancing the knowledge base of our profession in some meaningful way and the application of novel literature and existing practices into new settings are both exemplary ways of accomplishing this.

*An Area of Deficiency in the Professional Literature.* Because music therapy practice is constantly evolving, there will always be gaps in our professional literature. Identifying gaps that your particular skills and knowledge are suited to filling is an excellent way of developing a topic. Examples of contemporary areas of need in music therapy are as varied as technical musical analyses, outcome studies, and studies of group process with musical correlates. The point is that each one of us is especially suited to making significant and unique contributions to our profession based on our unique backgrounds, knowledge, and areas of expertise. Discovering what we have to uniquely offer the profession ensures that our contributions stem from our individual concerns while enhancing the diversity of the knowledge base of music therapy.

**Developing a Focus**

Often the focus is embedded in our topic. It is the reason we have chosen that topic and in such cases we do not have to address the issue of developing a focus. However, at other times we are drawn to a topic but are not sure why, we are given a topic and must develop the focus, or we engage in research in which the topic is preselected but the focus evolves. Thus, we are in the position of developing a focus for a given topic. Finding answers to the following categories of questions can guide us to the particular focus:

1) What drew me to this topic? Why do I want to study/discuss this group/individual/clinical approach?

2) What subject will be most meaningful for
   the individuals participating in the therapy?
   me as the author/presenter/therapist?
   the profession of music therapy?
   people in a position to provide access to music therapy services?

3) What is most unique about this approach/course of treatment?
   What is best exemplified here?
   What have I experienced here in a most profound or clear way?

4) What is most universal here? What can I discuss that will be of relevance to a broad range of clients/therapist?

In sum, focuses can evolve. This as okay and even desirable when it reflects the way in which our knowledge increases. As we prepare a presentation, lecture, or publication, we gain more insight into the subject we are discussing and the evolution of focus should reflect our increased knowledge. But it is important to be able to articulate (to ourselves) the focus as separate from the topic. This helps us to organize and sequence our material, choose the most appropriate vehicles for the presentation of information, and be clear about what we want our audience to take from the experience. Being able to articulate the figure and ground of our communications, something illustrated by the concepts of focus and topic respectively, is essential to the creation of successful publications and presentations.

CHAPTER 3

# Differences Between Writing and Presenting

There are many important differences between presenting and writing. Gaining insight into these differences can help us decide if a particular topic is best conveyed by writing or by presenting, and it can assist us in tailoring a piece of work for either presenting or publication. At times a publication begins life as a presentation and articulating the differences between the two mediums helps us to turn presentations into publications.

## Practical Considerations

In determining the appropriate form for communicating a given body of information, the first area to consider is its complexity. In a written work the reader controls the pacing of information and is able to stop, reread difficult sections, and look up supportive material and references. Hence, publications are better suited to complex topics needing reflection, analysis, and reinterpretation. In a presentation the presenter controls the pacing of information and the context of delivery. Hence, this form is better suited to more easily grasped material.

Presentations are more limited in scope and reach less people and a more homogenous audience than do publications. Publications reach a larger and more diverse audience. In contrast to presentations, writings can be translated and accessible to those who can read English but not understand spoken English. Thus, if reaching an international audience is a priority, publications offer a better opportunity to do so. And while publications and presentations can both have a profound impact, writings lend themselves to being revisited and reinterpreted over time by the reader.

It is also important to consider the volume of information you need to impart in order to best communicate your message. Different publications comprise vastly different volumes of information. A typical book chapter or journal article can range in length from 5–30 pages. A monograph is typically in the range of 30–100 pages. And a book contains 100 pages or more. When we present our work, typical lengths of time at a conference vary from 30, 60, 75, or 90 minutes in a presentation to five hours in a CMTE course. In developing some comparisons, consider that a recent issue of *Music Therapy Perspectives* contained articles that averaged approximately 9–10 pages in length. Each page takes approximately 6½ minutes to read aloud. Thus a typical journal article has a volume of information approximately equivalent to a 60-minute presentation.

## Scholarly Considerations

Those ideas, discoveries, definitions, and claims to knowledge that are written become part of the foundation of communal knowledge. Because of their permanence and the fact that they remain accessible for long durations of time, written communications define a domain. An idea may be discussed for many years among practitioners in a domain, but until it is published it is malleable and evolving. Once published it can continue to evolve, but its origins become identified with a time and a specific person or group.

This is important to discuss because writing does two things simultaneously: Through publishing, an idea becomes connected to a specific individual and sets one's identity in relation to one's colleagues; it is an act of self-declaration as one becomes identified with a particular idea or set of ideas. This may be difficult for some people and may serve to inhibit them from writing. Most of us are constantly evolving in our professional practices and belief systems and to become identified with a particular idea is to remain tethered to that idea (in the eyes of others) for the duration of one's professional career. Even if a publication ceases to be prevalent in the literature, once a person is identified with an idea or a way of thinking our tendency is to maintain that connection in our minds until it is replaced by something else. Among music therapy colleagues who have published significant works I do not think there is one who has not said, upon my commenting on their publication, some variation of "Well, I don't really think that way anymore. It's taken so many years to get that book/article/thesis/dissertation into print that I no longer agree with everything that I am saying!" As most writers know, past writings can cause as many difficulties as opportunities that they may bring. And most writers do not return to a given work, preferring to define themselves through future publications rather than through revisions of older publications.

More than those who do not write would assume, the primary purpose of any kind of writing is to perform a service to music therapy. The fact is, we do not write primarily for egocentric reasons to claim ideas as our own, primarily because of the phenomenon I have just noted. Even though an author may no longer subscribe to a particular idea as it is formulated in a publication, it is highly probable that putting the idea into the professional sphere provides conceptual tools to music therapists with which they can discuss their work. My primary belief is that the author serves as the vehicle for the idea to become manifest more than the idea is a vehicle for the author to attain renown. Thus, writers serve an important purpose by putting various ideas into the professional discourse and allowing the ideas to dialogue with one another. That a particular author no longer agrees with an idea he may have once written about is not important in the least; what is important is that the idea becomes available publicly for the use of all music therapists so that it can be used in dialogue for the advancement of the profession.

Just as a published idea identifies a writer, it simultaneously identifies the idea as the possession of the author who assumes the right to define it. This may not appear equitable as the writer may not be the person who coined a particular term and it may have been in public use for many years prior to being explicitly defined in a publication. In these cases, it is helpful for the writer to discuss some of the evolution of the term's use. This serves an important historical function and brings recognition to individuals who have contributed to professional discourse in ways other than writing. However, the writer is under no obligation to present a formulation of the term or concept that must be consistent with the prior, unpublished usages. As will be discussed below, an idea put into print carries greater weight and goes through more extensive checks and balances than does an idea that is discussed in other professional venues. The published version does become the definitive version for both practical and formal reasons: practical because it is the version of an idea that most people come into contact with and thus can reference in their own publications, presentations, and informal discussions; formal because the review that a published idea goes through endows the published version of an idea with a greater claim to knowledge.

In contrast to the relative permanence of published information, presentations are more suitable for information of a more transient nature. Presentations are professionally citable, but in general they are geared to more "in process" thinking than are publications. The material in presentations can be continually revisited by the presenter over many years as a particular framework is enhanced and becomes increasingly differentiated.

Scholarly standards for writing and publications differ and this leads to different types of associated knowledge claims.[1]

Conference presentations are citable in publications, although it may be difficult for readers to access unpublished papers. This becomes an easier task when the contents of presentations are published in proceedings books. At a conference, the sponsoring organization reviews the topic, a summary of the presentation, and the credentials of the presenter. But the actual material presented is not subject to an in-depth peer review. Therefore, the knowledge claims of material in presentations lie somewhere in between those of a chapter in an edited book and a journal article.

The various publication forms have different levels of review and therefore different levels of status in terms of the information presented. In books and monographs, typically the author is solely responsible for the content as most publishers do not assume a review function. However, sometimes a publisher will present a text to professional colleagues in an informal review process. More typical is when an author will share drafts of a book with professional peers in order to check the veracity and comprehensiveness of the material along with the intelligibility of the writing. Most responsible writers find this type of informal peer review to be essential and it is highly recommended. However, even with the informal review the content of a book is ultimately the responsibility of one person, the author, and this must be considered in evaluating the knowledge claims. The one exception here are texts which are based on qualitative research studies. While these texts also are the responsibility of the author, qualitative researchers often utilize methodological procedures that involve checking their conclusions with either research participants or outside auditors. In such cases, the conclusions have a stronger knowledge claim than do those of a nonresearch-based book, or a researched book without any type of methodological check on the findings.

In the case of chapters in edited books, the chapter author and book editor share responsibility for the veracity of the content. The relative weight of responsibility varies according to how active the editor is in influencing the content of the book chapter. This varies greatly among edited collections and no assumptions can be made regarding the editor's role in shaping the

[1] It is important to note that the ideas in this section reflect the present author's thinking and are not taken from any official guidelines, such as those of a professional association or scholarly body.

final content. Some editors take a very proactive role in influencing the content of the chapter, and others are much more passive, reserving their work for editorial and stylistic concerns.

Journal articles are another matter and in some ways the mechanisms of scholarly review and publication are the foundation of knowledge claims in academic disciplines. Peer reviewed journal articles are subject to a higher degree of scrutiny than are any other scholarly publications. The sponsoring organization, editorial board, editor, and article author all share responsibility for the veracity of content. The fact that this is the most rigorous review process means that journal articles possess the firmest knowledge claims.

Scholarly and professional organizations are much more selective in what they offer as publications than what they offer as presentations. Because the standards for publishing are higher, opportunities are more scarce, and as you determine the appropriate venues for your own communications you should keep these considerations in mind.

### Writing and Presenting: Concluding Thoughts

In going about the process of deciding if you should focus your efforts on writing or presenting, I suggest that you examine the nature of the information you would like to share. Is it complex and would an audience benefit from the opportunity for reflecting upon the presentation of ideas as they unfold? Is it something you have thought a great deal about and feel expert in? Does it fill an important gap in the professional literature? And is it something that you are comfortable being identified with professionally? If you can answer positively to these questions then I would suggest that writing would be the appropriate choice. Alternately, would the presentation of the information you are trying to get across benefit from direct contact with your audience? Is it a topic you are in the process of clarifying for yourself? And importantly, would it be difficult to secure the appropriate publishing venue? An affirmative answer to these questions suggests that presenting the material would be the appropriate choice.

A last word on this topic: The structure of the this publication suggests that presentations and publications are very different forms of communications. However, as I mentioned previously, presentations can often evolve into publications. The less stringent demands and standards for presentations as compared to publications allows you to offer material and test it for clarity. By presenting ideas and responding to the questions of an audience your own thoughts are sharpened and become better elaborated. You become more familiar and get more insight into it each time you present. This type of reworking of material in response to professional feedback is a type of peer review that helps take a vague set of related ideas and shape them into an extremely valuable professional contribution.

CHAPTER 4

# Writing

*Write in a way that draws the reader's attention to the sense and substance of the writing, rather than to the mood and temper of the author. If the writing is solid and good, the mood and temper of the writer will eventually be revealed and not at the expense of the work. Therefore, the first piece of advice is this: to achieve style, begin by affecting none.*

—E.B. White, *The Elements of Style*

### Issues in Scholarly Writing in Music Therapy

Let me state my belief at the outset of this discussion that *writing reflects thinking*. Some people genuinely have emotional blocks about writing. But for most people with an aversion to writing, a writing block is really a "thinking block." The common idea is that thinking is done purely mentally and the writing is an end product. This inhibits many people from attempting to express themselves and make a professional contribution through writing.

In fact, working on our writing is simultaneously working on our thinking. Hence, writing is like creating music in one way. We can start from a small element (single idea or melody) and create a much larger work, but the larger work is spun out in the realizing on paper. It is not preconceived and then put down on paper. So while many of us may feel intimidated about writing, I believe that this intimidation is more often due to an insecurity regarding the quality, comprehensiveness, importance, and relevance of one's ideas rather than inability to write per se. Once the source of one's reluctance is identified it becomes easier to overcome the obstacle.

That being said, there are some specific issues around writing for musicians in general and music therapists specifically. Some of us are music therapists because of a preference for musical expression over verbal expression. As a result, verbal expression becomes an undeveloped area of professional expertise. This leaves the public portrait of the profession to those music therapists more comfortable with words, something that can lead to a limited representation of the profession. A complete portrait of the profession requires the presence of all voices in our publications and conference presentations. And it is this desire for a more representative literature base and conference program that is one of the prime motivations I have had in putting this publication together.

There are many reasons why music therapists can find it difficult to write. Because our medium is music, we often hear colleagues say that words cannot capture our musical and clinical experiences. Or we hear that a significant component of the music therapy process is related to feeling and intuition, areas which some consider to be unsuited for professional discourse. However, many human experiences are nonverbal and music is not unique in this regard. Is it any harder to describe how chocolate ice cream tastes than it is to describe our experience of a piece of music? And we can develop specialized forms for communicating aspects of our experience that we want to include in professional communications that words do not represent well.

Moreover, standards for professional discourse can and do change. We can take an active role in changing them by supporting the importance of aesthetic, affective, intuitive, and musical factors in a systematic, scholarly, grounded, and professional way. And in fact, we have an obligation to do so if we believe that a profession more open to such professional discourse will enhance the quality of services offered to clients. So if you cannot relate to the predominant models of scholarly writing and feel that scholarly requirements place too many constraints on what you would like to say professionally, please keep in mind that these can change by your active participation. Find the models of writing that you can emulate and build upon them.

Almost all types of writing include aesthetic considerations, including scholarly writing as well as literary writing. Some of the considerations are the same, such as pacing, clarity, exposition and development, and engagement of the reader. Many of the considerations in structuring a written professional work parallel those of structuring a written work of art.

Honing our writings is an artistic process and realizing this can make it more of an enjoyable activity. At its best, the activity of writing is not so difficult from creating music. Maybe there is more in common than we generally assume. After all, while they are both nonverbal mediums, we say that we "write" a piece of music, sharing a commonality with verbal expression, but we do not "write" a painting, for example. And when writing becomes a more pleasurable activity, this is often manifest in the final product.

There is always a rhetorical or persuasive function to our writing. Good publications should convey our ideas clearly while convincing others of their value. Writing is meant to be read and engaged in intellectually by others. Unless we believe in our ideas, and unless these ideas have a firm foundation, why would we want to publicize them and be identified with them? Some of us feel that writing is more of a sharing activity and our intentions should not be to convince people of our ideas but present them for their consideration. If they find them useful, that is fine, and if they do not find them useful, that is fine as well.

However, I think of ideas as children that we send off into the world. We provide our children with various kinds of emotional, physical, intellectual, and financial support. We do not expect our children to survive or flourish without this kind of support. Ideas are the same. If we value them, if they have been helpful to us, we should send them off into the world where ideas compete with each other with all of the support that we can muster. This is the nature of the symbiotic relationship between ideas and people. They help us in our work, enhance our awareness of what we do, give our work more meaning, and therefore enhance the quality of services we provide to clients. In return, we do all we can to help the ideas survive, flourish, and even evolve and change.

Yes, ideas are like children in more ways than one. Not only do we support them, we have to learn to let go of them as well, as they become a public possession through our writings. Writing involves putting our cherished ideas into the world where they create their own destinies, perhaps changing in such dramatic ways that we no longer recognize them. Once we accept this fact of writing (and parenting!) we become less inhibited in our writing.

Traditionally, the persuasive function of scholarly writing is not acknowledged. But in writing we are like a lawyer building a case based on the available evidence. Our ability to be persuasive operates within the constraints of the data in research or accepted forms of professional practice in clinical articles. These considerations give us more creative free reign in creating writing while also giving a direction and form to writings.

If you remain unconvinced of the importance of being convincing in your writings consider that there is always a rhetorical aspect to writing, no matter how hard we try to eliminate it. Paul Atkinson (1990) has noted that even the impersonal writing voice of the traditional experimental report in which the first person voice is completely absent is itself a rhetorical device. The impersonal voice of this writing suggests that the knowledge claims have greater authority because they are not the product of a fallible human being, an imperfect "I," but instead are the pronouncements of an impersonal, faceless authority.

**The Role of Colleagues in Scholarly Writing**

I would like to take the metaphor of publications as children one step further. While parents are ultimately responsible for the well-being and survival of their children, many other people contribute to their character as well. Relatives, teachers, friends, and various role models in society strongly influence the character of children as they move into the world. As parents, we have an obligation to expose our children to a diverse assortment of positive influences because no single person can possibly provide all things necessary for a child to grow into a well-rounded adult.

Similarly, I have found it to be invaluable to share drafts of publications with trusted colleagues prior to submitting them to journals or publishers. There are a number of reasons for doing this that relate to the style and content of the publication. However, the help provided by colleagues is not limited to offering constructive criticism. The positive reactions given by colleagues can provide the support and encouragement that we need to follow through with a publication and bring it to a satisfactory completion. So if you are in the position of offering prepublication reactions to a colleague, I encourage you to address the strengths of the publication as well as any deficiencies.

While copy editors do essential work, they cannot be expected to provide the type of feedback offered by professional colleagues. I have found that just about every type of professional publication will benefit from this type of feedback, particularly as it concerns the following areas: understandability, the use of examples, accuracy, comprehensiveness, and writing tone.

*Understandability.* As writers, we know what we mean to say and so it is difficult for us to judge how comprehensible our writing is. When we share our writings with colleagues within the same professional specialization and they find the writings to be obtuse or difficult to follow, it can be assumed that this is due to a problem in the writing rather than in the reader. So to ensure the comprehensibility of our writing it is essential that it be reviewed by readers with a better than average grasp of the subject matter.

If your target audience is the general music therapy audience rather than those with any special expertise or area of interest, you may also want to include such a person in the group of colleagues who comment upon your drafts.

*Use of Examples*. The use of examples is essential in scholarly writing and it performs at least three essential functions: substantiating empirical claims, illustrating ideas, and supporting a line of argument.

One of the hallmarks of scholarly writing is that empirical claims are substantiated, either through employing references to other works from which the claim is drawn or by giving examples that support the claim being made. When outside literature is used to substantiate a claim, there is little need for external feedback, unless of course the writer is mistaken. However, when examples are used to substantiate a claim, the degree to which such examples support the claim, and the number of examples needed to make one's case, are both matters of judgment and this is where it is essential to have opinions from outside readers. If readers who are naturally sympathetic to your point of view feel that your examples are somewhat shaky in supporting your point, you can be sure that the average reader will react in an even more skeptical way.

Many professional writings deal with ideas in a variety of forms, such as explanatory theories, treatment rationales, and conceptual arguments in support of various approaches to clinical treatment and the education and training of music therapists. Because writers are most comfortable with the ideas they have an affinity for, and because these are the ideas that most of us write about, it can be difficult to judge how many and what types of examples best illustrate the ideas that we are discussing. Outside readers can help us in making these judgments.

The same considerations come into play when an author presents a particular thesis or point of view and develops this perspective through an extended argument. The use of examples is an essential aspect of philosophical argument in general. They ground the argument in the experience of the writer and the reader and provide criteria against which the soundness of the argument can be measured. Again, whether or not a particular set of examples is convincing is best determined by a reader other than the author because of the fact that the latter is already convinced of the soundness of the argument.

*Accuracy.* Another hallmark of scholarly writing is making every effort to be accurate in our empirical statements. It is relatively easy for writers to check purely factual matters such as the number of professional music therapists, for example. However, there are other types of empirical claims about which there may be no objective statistic but upon which we would like to comment. Perhaps you want to make an observation about the similarities and differences in music therapy practice in different geographical locations, whether nationally or internationally. Anyone who has traveled relatively extensively can make such a pronouncement, and while it is not made arbitrarily, it is made without the type of documentation one would normally expect in a scholarly publication. At times, we need to make such judgments in our writings and often we can do so in an unproblematic way if we have sufficient knowledge about the area upon which we are commenting. However, all writers have had idiosyncratic professional and personal histories that lead to a unique set of categories of thinking, prejudices, and expectations. Hence, it can be invaluable to have colleagues comment upon such claims so that the writer can either soften or qualify the claim in order for it to be more accurate. The choice to make such observations absent strong published documentation requires the writer to check such claims against the perceptions of other authorities in the profession.

*Comprehensiveness.* In a sense, comprehensiveness is related to accuracy because it relates to rendering an inaccurate description by errors of omission rather than commission. Writers do this when they make global or unqualified pronouncements about music therapy and the statements are actually only relevant for certain types of music therapy practice.

Different types of publications are intended to cover different types of domains: an area or level of music therapy practice; a particular client population; or a particular model, intervention, or procedure. And all music therapists develop their own internal constructions about the profession in general based on their own experience. Although we have a scholarly obligation to employ published information when it is available, it is essential to draw upon the perspectives of others when we are making pronouncements based on experience. Remember, once you say something in print it becomes a citable reference for other scholars and authors. This brings an extraordinary obligation on the part of the writer to be as accurate and comprehensive as possible.

*Writing Tone.* All writers necessarily convey a tone through the way that they use words; this is one of the inevitabilities of writing. This tone or writing voice becomes the writer's public image for readers who only encounter the author through publications. The writer's voice is probably the single most important ingredient in engaging readers. A particular topic or title will attract readers to a publication, but it is the writer's voice that keeps them engaged.

In scholarly writing, the author should not try to disguise or hide the natural voice because what will be conveyed will be the sense of a person hiding behind words. Strunk & White (2000), authorities in the area of style and usage, note how "all writers, by the way they use the language, reveal something of their spirits, their habits, their capacities, and their biases. This is inevitable as well as enjoyable" (p. 67). Writers should endeavor to develop and employ writing voices that best serve their intentions as writers and the purposes behind particular publications.

Now for a little self-revelation on the part of the author. My academic training prior to becoming a music therapist was in philosophy. Hence, many of my interests are philosophical in nature and many of my writings employ the form of argument. At times, my writing can assume a polemical tone in which I am so focused upon being convincing about a particular point that I wind up alienating the reader. In these instances, my writing tone can serve to work counter to, and even undermine, the very purpose of the publication. But becoming aware of this tendency has allowed me to be less governed by it. And I have only become aware of it through the comments of colleagues who have examined early drafts of publications.

This does not mean that we cannot be disputatious in our professional writings. I actually believe that the profession of music therapy can benefit from a significantly greater amount of publications in which music therapists take up each other's positions and opinions and engage in healthy criticism; this is how academic disciplines grow. And I also do not think that all of our opinions should be qualified to such a degree that the forcefulness of our points suffers. The most fruitful balance to strike in writing about music therapy should be one in which our beliefs and opinions can be documented and stated with clarity and force in an engaging writing voice that invites the reader to entertain ideas and new categories of thinking that the reader might otherwise not be drawn to. Trusted colleagues are in the best position to help us understand when the writing voice of the author is either undermining or supporting the purposes behind the writing.

### The Use of Background Material in Structuring a Publication

There are number of questions that you should ask yourself as you prepare a professional publication. Foremost among these is *For whom am I writing and what background information do they need to understand what I am saying?* When engaging in professional writing, it is important to put oneself in the position of the potential reader or audience. This can be difficult at first because it means stepping back from what you want to say to consider how the message will be received. But it is essential to write with a particular audience in mind because this will help you to structure your publication.

Different potential audiences are as follows: anyone interested in your title; professional music therapists only; music therapy students and professionals; and particular music therapy professionals, such as those with a given level of expertise, a particular theoretical persuasion, or those who work in a specialized clinical area. Your answers here determine how much background information you need to include, the level of complexity of your presentation, what you can accomplish through the writing, and the language and tone of the presentation.

Background information provides the context for the main ideas of your publication and it is essential to provide the appropriate level of it. If you provide too much information, you run the risk of boring your audience and obscuring the main point of your writing. On the other hand, if you do not have a sufficient amount of background material, your audience may not be able to fully grasp the new material you present and link it to already existing practices and concepts. It is the writer's job not only to be intelligible but to also assist the reader in connecting the new material to the reader's existing knowledge base. Without this connection, the material may be understood, but not assimilated in a deep manner and thus soon forgotten. Of course, the various readers of any publication will have an individual blend of prior knowledge and interests; hence there is no single optimum amount of background information to provide.

Background information can provide context through both its breadth and its depth and a judicious use of background or supportive material can serve as the link between the reader's existing knowledge base and the new information that you are going to provide. For example, in doctoral and master's studies, this material is known as the "Related Literature." It serves the academic purpose of demonstrating the candidate's knowledge base while also providing the reader with the information needed to understand, evaluate, and apply the new material presented.

Two images that come to mind in describing the role of background material are a spectrum and a pyramid. Background material can be presented in a hierarchical manner, resembling a pyramid, as one moves from the general to the specific. For example, consider Katrina Skewes's (2001) doctoral dissertation entitled *The Experience of Group Music*

*Therapy for Six Bereaved Adolescents.* The sequence of her literature review, in part, is as follows:

Example 5.
Sequence and Components of a Literature Review

---

Selected Group Music Therapy Methods for Working with Adolescents
Adolescents in Music Therapy
The Relationship Between Adolescence and Music
Adolescence

Here we can see a progression from the general to the more specific—hence, the pyramid structure—so that the overall topic can be understood within the much more general area of interest regarding the nature of adolescence. It should be clear that there are no absolute criteria for determining how broad the pyramid should be at the base and how narrow at its apex. These decisions are made pragmatically and are influenced by scholarly considerations, such as the realm of application that the writer desires for the material, and pragmatic considerations such as the size of the publication. For each publication you should articulate the elements of what your pyramidic structure should contain based on your purposes and the needs of your envisioned audience.

In addition to the pyramid structure it is also important to locate the ideas in your publication on the professional spectrum of ideas and approaches. This is what I am considering breadth of knowledge rather than depth. For example, in Skewes (2001) there is a section on "Current Practice Music Therapy Group Improvisation." This section details a variety of improvisational approaches in group work so that Skewes's own approach can be understood in its clinical context. And just as the bottom and top of the pyramid has to be articulated, one also has to decide how broad a spectrum should be described. So Skewes did not include a review of all music therapy group theories, improvisational models, models of improvisation with individuals, or an historical review of improvisational models that may no longer be so prevalent. She defined the relevant context in terms of current group music therapy improvisational approaches and this dictated the scope of her writing.

In professional publications there may be external constraints or suggestions on the background information needed for a particular publication. For example, in journal articles it is very common for editorial board members to suggest, through the blind review process, the addition of a number of scholarly sources, references, and topics to be covered in an article. While these judgments are not arbitrary, there are still a number of idiosyncratic factors that come in to play when a person decides what the relevant context should be for an article, both in terms of depth and breadth. This is why it is essential that you know what your audience is and what you want to achieve through your publication. The journal reviewer or book editor might have a different agenda for your publication from you and that agenda may not be fully conscious. As you negotiate the final form of a publication with editors and reviewers it is important to keep in mind that there are many different contexts in which a single publication can be considered. It is essential for you to be fully aware of your target context so that you can argue for the inclusion of only that material which supports your agenda in writing.

A recent publication of the present author consists of a study which integrates text and video and is entitled *Playin' in the Band: A Qualitative Study of Popular Music Styles as Clinical Improvisation* (Aigen, 2002). In writing this study I had three different groups in mind, and while there certainly is overlap among the three, I nevertheless believed that the groups were distinct enough to be conceived of separately: music therapists who are familiar with popular musical styles and want to learn more about how to implement and conceptualize their use in improvisation; music therapists who may not know much about applications of popular styles in music thearpy; and music therapists interested in the Nordoff-Robbins approach but who may not be aware of its application in the domain of popular styles.

For all of these groups, I was interested in showing how clinical music therapy approaches can dovetail with nonclinical uses of music and I was interested in placing the use of the popular styles in therapy on a continuum with their use in nonclinical settings. In terms of language used, in this study I used many terms such as "groove, "jamming," and "turnaround" that are familiar to pop musicians but that may not be familiar to others. Because part of my agenda was to illustrate the clinical function of authentic renditions of these styles I felt that it was important to do so within the conceptual system indigenous to those styles. I also wanted to legitimize the use of such terminology as being just as useful as more traditional musical terms.

In the area of background information, something that I discussed in this publication was the improvisational tradition in rock music because I believed that not many people are aware of it. I discussed the origins of improvising (or jamming) in rock in the decade of the 1960s and observed how it has continued to the present day in the jam band genre. Thus, rather than contextualize the work in terms of existing music therapy models of improvisation, in this study I felt the relevant context was nonclinical uses of improvisational rock music which shared many of the interactional characteristics of the clinical music. My choice of background information was dictated by my overall agenda which was to highlight many of the parallels between clinical and nonclinical uses of music.

This is an example of considering what information the reader will require to come to the conclusion I would like to illustrate. Recall that earlier in this paper it was discussed that in the advocacy model of professional communications it is permissible—even necessary, some would argue—to have a particular point of view that one is either explicitly or implicitly promoting. Being aware of your point of view, and understanding how you are structuring a publication to best communicate it, means that you not only have to consider what information to provide but also what type of information will be most convincing to your intended audience. For example, if you are writing about a particular clinical approach, you may need to include quantitative data, a strong theoretical foundation, testimony about its efficacy from clients or caregivers, supportive media such as video or audio recordings, detailed descriptions of interventions, or connections to previously published forms of practice. Obviously, all writings cannot contain all of these, so remember that the components of your writing should be dictated by your purposes, not by convention.

In deciding what form of writing will best suit your purpose there are a few considerations. The first is how much information you have to share and how much supportive material is required for its exposition. Briefer publications can take the form of a journal article, a book chapter, or an unpublished manuscript. A moderate amount of information can be presented in a monograph and longer expositions require a book form.

It is also important to consider the constraints that you can publish within. If you do not want to have to meet any external requirements you are limited to unpublished manuscripts or perhaps self-published books. Typically, published monographs or books have a minimal level of external constraints to meet, although this will vary depending upon whether you are searching for a publisher for an already written work, or you are shopping a book idea among publishers. Publishers typically do not exercise the type of editorial review and control over content that is more true of professional organizations, for example.

When you are writing a chapter in an edited book, there are more editorial constraints to meet. Typically, an editor takes a fair amount of responsibility for the content of an edited book and so is free to exercise some editorial control. This, however, varies greatly among editors. My experience has been that edited collections that are intended for use in academic settings tend to be written with a far greater degree of influence by the editor than are collections which are geared to a more advanced reader or that result from the proceedings of a conference or symposium. Chapters in books created for a student audience often have a structural homogeneity that makes comparisons among topics easier and facilitates use of the text in college courses.

The most significant constraints one meets is in publishing journal articles. Peer-reviewed journals are responsible for their content and they institutionalize review practices which ensure that what is published is considered well documented and supported by experts in the area. This is the nature of the review process, although there is a great variety in the types of editorial control exercised in scholarly journals. If you have an interest in publishing articles that push novel viewpoints or that extend traditional writing forms you have two choices: 1) attempt to publish in more conventional journals in order to help effect an evolution of style or content; and 2) seek publication in those journals whose previously published contents seem congruent with the way that you would like to write.

## Creating a Writing Guide

Something that I create for every publication is what I call a "writing guide." This is true for publications as diverse as a voluminous research study, a clinical case study, or a brief book chapter or journal article on clinical theory or research methodology. From the outset of any project that I engage in, I am thinking about the various ways to present the information that I am gathering.

The writing guide is more than just an outline or writing plan, but it may contain these elements. The guide is not done at one time. Instead, it is an ongoing work in which I collect my thoughts regarding a particular publication over time. It is a place where I can talk to myself or think on paper and it includes a number of elements:

Table 8.
Components of a Writing Guide

| |
|---|
| Ideas about the components of a project |
| Ideas about the purposes behind the writing |
| Ideas about narrative devices and presentational structures |
| Ideas about the sequence of elements |
| Ideas about how to bridge the various sections of a publication |

It has been my experience that the topic, focus, structure, and content of any publication evolve. We need a place to engage in the creative conceptualization of our writings and to collect our own inspirations as we compose a written work. And because good publications tend to take on a life of their own, and hence suggest new elements and devices as they emerge, it is essential to have a vehicle in which to allow our conceptualizations to evolve in a systematic way.

In engaging in the process of creating a writing guide it is important not to censor yourself. Just sit down and write! Also, do not restrict your imagination as the specifics of the project can be honed later on. In the writing guide, I focus on discussing what I want to write about, what sources of information I might include, who my audience is, and what form(s) my writing might take. It is also important to revisit the guide as you get deeper into a project. Do not be afraid to change it. Remember that it should change if you are learning more as you put your publication together. The guide is a place to start but is not a plan to be rigidly followed because the actual piece of writing, as it emerges, will have its own internal logic. This can (and should) supercede the guide.

## Style Guides and Other Aids to Writing

As a youth in school there was probably no aspect of education that I liked more than reading literature, and no aspect that I liked less than studying grammar and word usage. The two activities seemed so different from one another that I wondered why they were normally taught in the same class simply called "English." However, a funny thing has happened to me as a professional music therapist who finds himself living so much in the world of words: I have grown to greatly enjoy the study of writing, both in terms of developing a writing voice and in terms of learning to write correctly. The significant change for me was in learning how the two aspects of writing are intimately connected. I now see how learning to write concisely, clearly, and grammatically are essential in creating publications that are not only comprehensible but stimulating as well.

All writers require assistance in creating their publications, a task that normally falls to editors. But prior to submitting a publication to an editor—whether this is a member of a journal editorial board, an editor of a book with many contributors, or a copy editor employed by a publisher—it is incumbent upon writers to ensure that their writing is appropriate for scholarly publications in terms of its style and content.

There are a large number of publications available to assist writers, and they fall into five general categories according to their primary purpose. In each category, I will discuss a few publications that I have found to be most helpful, although there are many other options available to readers.

Table 9. Categories of Books About Writing

1) Writing Style and Grammar Guides
2) Guides to Conventions in Scholarly Publishing
3) Guides to Book Formatting and Preparing Books for Publication
4) Dissertation and Thesis Guides
5) Books About Writing, Language, and their Relationship to Social Realities

Writing Style and Grammar Guides. In any type of professional, scholarly writing there is no more important consideration than writing clearly and correctly. This is true for a number of reasons. It shows that we respect both our subject matter and our readers; it makes it easier for reviewers, editors, publishers, and professors to focus on the content of our writing; it ensures that the meanings that we intend are conveyed to readers; and, it elevates the profession of music therapy.

The publication that I recommend most highly in this area is Strunk and White's (2000) *The Elements of Style.* Since its first printing in 1959 millions of writers (and their readers) have benefited from this little book—85 pages in a format that fits in a back pocket—that includes rules of usage, principles of composition, commonly misused words and expressions, and an approach to style. The book is written so engagingly, so succinctly, and with such clarity that it is actually enjoyable to read. Moreover, its contents are all linked to the purpose of writing: enhanced communication. Consider the following example on the merits of concision, itself a paradigm of brevity:

> Vigorous writing is concise. A sentence should contain no unnecessary words, a paragraph no unnecessary sentences, for the same reason that a drawing should have no unnecessary lines and a machine no unnecessary parts. This requires not that the writer make all sentences short, or avoid all detail and treat subjects only in outline, but that every word tell. (Strunk & White, 2000, p. 23)

Beginning writers (and some experienced ones as well) tend not to pay sufficient attention to their grammar and word usage and scholarly writing suffers as a result. The ease of self-publishing and the move to having authors providing camera-ready copy to publishers means that increasing numbers of publications are made available that are not subject to the scrutiny of professional copy editors. Therefore, it is incumbent upon writers to develop expertise in editing their publications. If you value your own writing, and if you want to give it every chance to be published, you should endeavor to make it as correct as possible. It is as mistaken to think that the content and form of a publication can be separated as it is to imagine that an incorrect note value does not alter a musical score in some essential way.

Guides to Conventions in Scholarly Publishing. Contrary to what many readers might assume, there are a number of different traditions in scholarly publishing regarding topics such as how published works are cited in a text, footnotes are employed, reference lists are formatted, and tables and figures are labeled. However, the predominance of scholarly journals to which music therapists tend to submit articles follow the guidelines of the *Publication Manual of the American Psychological Association* (2001), otherwise known as the APA Manual. For this reason, many music therapy publications, e.g. books and dissertations, also tend to employ APA guidelines, although there is no necessity to do so.

The APA manual covers much more than just the correct way to cite a published work in the body of the text. Topics that it covers include, among others, the content and organization of manuscripts, writing style and reducing bias in language, general editorial style regarding punctuation and headings, and the preparation of a reference list. It is essential to use APA publishing conventions if you are writing an article for submission to a scholarly journal. If you are writing a book or a chapter in an edited book it is likely that you will be required to follow APA form as well, so it behooves all writers to become familiar with these guidelines. An important note here: The APA Manual is currently in its fifth edition and the guidelines can change significantly from one edition to the next. Major edition changes occur every decade with more minor revisions taking place in between these intervals. In your publications, make sure that you are following the most current edition of the manual.

As was mentioned previously, there are alternatives to APA form and if you are writing a thesis or dissertation you should determine your university's policy on the usage of alternative style guides. It may be that if your publication is more historical, philosophical, or biographical in nature, it would be more appropriate to use a different style guide. Other well-known style guides include *The Chicago Manual of Style* (University of Chicago Press, 1993) and *The MLA* [Modern Language Association] *Style Manual* (Achtert & Gibaldi, 1985). Whichever manual you choose I have two recommendations: First, be sure that the manual you choose is acceptable to whomever you are submitting your work for publication. Second, make this decision *prior to* beginning your writing. There are few things more time consuming and disconcerting than having to make significant changes in style and reference format once a work is completed, especially if the work is a long one such as a book or doctoral dissertation.

Guides to Book Formatting and Preparing Books for Publication. Publications such as books and monographs can be provided to publishers in one of two basic forms: either as a raw text or disc that is then formatted as a book by the publisher, or in the form of camera-ready copy. When publishers ask for camera-ready copy this means that the final published book will look exactly as it is provided to the publisher by the author or editor. The published work may be provided on paper or on a computer disk and the publisher makes no changes in its appearance.

Providing camera-ready copy has advantages to both the author and the publisher. For the former, this puts total control over the appearance of the book in the author's hands. It also allows the book to be brought into publication much quicker than if raw text is provided. Typically this can happen in a matter of six to eight weeks rather than the six months to two years that can typify book contracts where the author is providing raw text. The primary advantage to the publisher is the saving of expenses related to turning raw text into a publishable form.

There are also disadvantages to both parties. For the author, there are two considerations here. First, providing camera-ready copy is significantly more time consuming than is providing raw text. Until you have done so, it is impossible to imagine the amount of work in preparing a book for publication and I do not recommend doing so unless your word processing skills are well above average. Thus, some of the time saved in bringing a book to publication by supplying camera-ready text is lost due to the investment of time required to do this type of formatting. Also, the look of the book is limited by the options offered in basic word processing programs. While programs such as Microsoft Word and Corel WordPerfect provide a number of attractive options in formatting a book, their products are not equivalent to what can be done by a professional publisher. The same factors are disadvantages to the publisher as well. The final appearance of the book may not be up to the standards of other books in the publisher's catalogue and the publisher might have a publication schedule disrupted by unforeseen delays in the author's work of preparing the book for publication.

An essential book for authors, especially those who are asked to prepare camera-ready copy for publishers, is *The Chicago Manual of Style* (University of Chicago Press, 1993). This work includes may of the style, usage, and referencing issues addressed by both Strunk and White (2000) and the APA Manual (2001) but goes well beyond these topics in its 900-plus pages to address every aspect of making a book, from the correct order of the "front matter," e.g. foreword, preface, acknowledgments, etc., to the format for running heads, those small titles adjacent to page numbers on book pages. Many more topics are addressed in the book than will be of interest to most authors, and you can be certain that any question you have regarding formatting or usage will be answered in its pages.

Most of the publishing conventions that music therapists are familiar with come from the formatting requirements for the submission of academic papers or scholarly journal articles. The problem is that most of these conventions do not make for very attractive books. This is why it essential to have access to a work such as *The Chicago Manual.* As someone who has gone through the process of preparing camera-ready text on a number of occasions, I have three recommendations for authors preparing to do the same: 1) master your particular word processing program prior to beginning the formatting of your book; 2) study other books whose design and layout you find to be particularly attractive and pattern your own book after those that you admire; and 3) focus upon creating a simple but elegant design whenever you have choices to make. Think of the design as a form of architecture in which the choices you make have both an aesthetic and functional purpose that should come together in enhancing the essential messages of the book.

Dissertation and Thesis Guides. Although many of the topics addressed in the present book are applicable to dissertations and theses, these academic papers are not addressed specifically because of the present focus on professional communications. However, there are scores of books written to assist graduate students to successfully complete dissertations and theses.[1] Many of these books offer practical help in overcoming the obstacles that prevent people from completing these works in a timely way. Rather than recommending a particular publication, I suggest that you go to your local bookstore and skim the many publications there in order to find one whose tone you find engaging and whose contents address the particular areas in which you would like assistance.

I will, however, briefly mention two works. First, is *A Manual for Writers of Term Papers, Theses, and Dissertations* by Kate L. Turabian (1987). This book is published by the University of Chicago Press and is useful in formatting footnotes, endnotes, text citations, reference lists, and bibliographies. It is more of the nature of a style guide than it is an aid to writing a dissertation and it offers an alternative to some of the style guides mentioned above.

Also of note is a publication by two music therapists, Gary Ansdell and Mercédès Pavlicevic (2001), *Beginning Research in the Arts Therapies: A Practical Guide.* As the title indicates, this book is oriented toward assisting beginning researchers, not writers per se. However, many of the topics addressed are quite relevant for authors of all types of works, and because the text is directed specifically to arts therapists, the content of the examples used throughout the text will be directly relevant for music therapists. There are a variety of topics in this publication that are not specific to preparing research publications: developing focuses; choosing titles and exploring the meaning behind the way titles are phrased; reading, reviewing, and summarizing existing literature to find gaps in knowledge; reading in an academically critical manner; bringing style and structure to writing; and, organizing a literature review. The authors also present a model of writing based on the sonata form structure of exposition, development, recapitulation, and coda.

---

[1] In the United States a dissertation is completed at the doctoral level and the thesis at the master's level. In European universities the doctoral study is referred to as a thesis.

The artistic function of these movements is connected to the cognitive function of introducing and arguing the basic themes of publication.

Ansdell and Pavlicevic conclude with an elaboration of David Aldridge's (1999) idea of a "community of inquirers," a notion that embraces the "vibrancy of interacting with other professionals through writing" (Ansdell & Pavlicevic, 2001, p. 243). Aldridge is interested in promoting the development of music therapy through enhancing communication among the worldwide community of researchers. To this end, he stresses the "urgency of training . . . writing and presentation skills" (p. 26) and readers interested in gaining a broader perspective on the function of professional communications in the research arena are directed to Aldridge's article.

<u>Books About Writing, Language, and Their Relationship to Social Realities</u>. A final category of books on writing comprises a variety of topics, most of which are being written by qualitative researchers. There are a few reasons for this focus on writing among such researchers: many qualitative researchers are interested in applying narrative forms from literature in order to better convey their findings; qualitative reports tend to be quite long and complex, thus requiring different types of writing skills from those in many quantitative research reports; qualitative researchers maintain a stance of reflexivity about their activities, thus necessitating an examination of the way that writing up the research report helps determine the nature of the findings; and many qualitative research reports include voluminous amounts of verbal data in the form of interview transcripts and data logs—working with verbal material as data stimulates thoughts on how the various ways words are used influences our perceptions and constructions of reality. As you can see from this sample of reasons behind the focus on language and writing, the issues addressed by qualitative researchers, although arising from their research work, has implications for all types of scholarly writing.

If you have an interest in these types of books—and I highly recommend examining them regardless of the type of professional writing that you are doing—a good place to begin is Harry F. Wolcott's (1990) *Writing Up Qualitative Research.* This smallish monograph addresses practical and conceptual problems in writing and many of the suggestions are applicable to any type of writing. These include areas such as how to plan and structure a publication, when to share the manuscript, the difference between revising and editing, and how to keep going when obstacles are encountered. The suggestions come directly from the author's experience and are presented in an immediately accessible way. Some of the central topics of the present publication were stimulated by Wolcott's writing.

A comprehensive text that addresses many aspects of writing in a lively, engaging, and stimulating manner is *On Writing Qualitative Research: Living by Words* by Margot Ely, Ruth Vinz, Maryann Downing, and Margaret Anzul (1997). The book discusses general issues about writing qualitative research, the broad spectrum of literary devices being applied in research reports, ways to integrate creative writing approaches in some of the seemingly mundane components of publications such as outlines and tables of contents, writing in analytic and interpretive modes, practical issues such as negotiating with journal editors and referees, and the ways in which writing can transform the self, the latter a topic of inherent interest for therapists. This book is extraordinarily entertaining for a scholarly book and is an excellent representative of the type of writing it exists to foster among researchers and other scholarly and professional writers.

The publications of Paul Atkinson (1990, 1992) focus on the interaction between how language is used and how research findings are generated, reported, and ultimately, understood by readers. Readers wishing to dip into this area of scholarly investigation are directed to his 1992 monograph, *Understanding Ethnographic Texts,* the central issue of which is a brief examination of the paradox that making ethnographic reports readable renders them less than recognizable by those individuals who are most intimately involved in the field of study. In his 1992 book, *The Ethnographic Imagination: Textual Constructions of Reality,* Atkinson takes up the notion that "texts do not simply and transparently report an independent order of reality. Rather, the texts themselves are implicated in the work of reality-construction" (p. 7).

While Atkinson focuses on the conventions of ethnographic texts—a particular type of qualitative research—his general point is that all publications utilize narrative strategies to make their arguments and influence the construal of the realities they represent. As was previously noted, even the standard impersonal writing voice of the traditional scientific report is seen not as the absence of rhetoric but as an example of a particular rhetorical strategy. The absence of the first-person voice endows such "impersonal" reports with an air of authority not present in research reports that are contextualized within first-person accounts.

Atkinson (1992) argues that all aspects of writing reflect epistemological biases. In a passage particularly relevant for the topic of the present work, he refers to Bazerman's analysis of the APA publication manual in which "he shows how a set of behaviourist assumptions have become increasingly taken for granted and inscribed in the required formats of APA style. . . . The APA style . . . is one of the restricted range of acceptable styles that place constraints—in some cases quite severe—on what is to count as a well-formed scholarly representation" (cited in Atkinson, p. 50). This observation explains why it is primarily qualitative researchers operating from alternative epistemological frameworks who have been attempting to expand the range of types of writing considered to be appropriate in scholarly and professional venues.

Readers with an interest in the unique challenges and conditions involved in describing music therapy processes are directed to Gary Ansdell's (1999) study, *Music Therapy as Discourse and Discipline: A Study of "Music Therapist's" Dilemma*. Ansdell draws upon constructs from musicology, semiotics, and discourse analysis to examine how music therapists talk and write about music therapy, and how these various domains and means of verbalization help determine the way the music therapy is described and theorized about within the tradition of Nordoff-Robbins music therapy.

The work is recommended for readers with a strong interest in the interface of words and music, particularly as it impacts theorizing and description of music therapy process in any professional venue. Ansdell examines the way that words are used at three levels increasingly distant from the actual experience: discussing recordings of music therapy sessions, discussing general themes in a staff meeting setting, and examining the use of language in a number of publications about music therapy. While the context for the research is a particular model of music therapy practice, the conclusions of the study are relevant to the profession of music therapy in general because the study did not focus on the interaction of words and music in the sessions, but upon the way that words are used among professionals.

Although it does not fit neatly into any of the categories of books just described, one final publication to discuss in this area is *Music Therapy Research: Quantitative and Qualitative Perspectives,* edited by Barbara Wheeler (1995a). Research is a professional activity that reaches completion when it is shared with colleagues. There is an interaction between research activities and the forms and venues in which research is brought to an audience. Thus, anyone who engages in research must also consider the most suitable form to disseminate research findings and thus grapple with many of the issues around communicating with colleagues.

Four chapters in Wheeler's text deal with issues that are also considered in the present text. Although the topics are approached in terms of their relevance for quantitative research, there are enough commonalities among all forms of writing to make some of the content applicable beyond that domain. Readers are directed to Kenneth Bruscia's (1995b) chapter on "Topics and Questions in Quantitative Research," Barbara Wheeler's (1995b) chapter on "Developing a Topic," Cheryl Dileo Maranto's (1995) chapter on "Reviewing the Literature," and Michael McGuire's (1995) chapter on "Writing the Research Report."

## Publication Forms

### *Unpublished Manuscripts*

This is an underutilized form of communications in the music therapy community. Although the circulation of unpublished manuscripts does not seem to be prevalent among music therapists, it can be very useful for informal communications. It has many advantages over other forms of publication.

There is an immediacy of communication that is unmatched by any other type of writing. Through the use of computers and e-mail we can complete a publication and immediately put it in the possession of anyone. There is absolutely no time lag between the formulation of your ideas and their dissemination, something unheard of previously. This can be important when the information we want to provide to others would benefit from a timely distribution. An example would be papers focusing on work with victims of various kinds of disasters. There is often an acute need for this type of assistance at a specific moment in time.

Also, as the author and disseminator of the publication you have initial control over who has access to the publication. Thus you can provide the publication to individuals that you imagine would be interested in the material, targeting your audience in a very specific way. Of course, making your publication available in an electronic forms means that it can be disseminated universally and you have absolutely no control over the various individuals it is sent to. And you have no control over any alterations it may pick up along the way for which you may be deemed responsible. This is certainly a potential drawback.

As the author and disseminator of the publication you have complete control over its length and contents, barring any kind of unauthorized changes. This can be an advantage for works of a length that may not be suitable for other forms of publication, such as those that are either too brief or too long for a journal article. The same considerations go for content. Perhaps you have some ideas that you have been playing with that you may not be ready to publish formally, either because they are not yet worked out in detail, not yet sufficiently substantiated, or just not suitable for a professional publication. In an unpublished manuscript you can formulate and disseminate ideas to your colleagues that do not have to meet any external constraints or standards. Of course, the disadvantage is that because there is absolutely no review of the material in an unpublished manuscript—either by an editorial board, book editor, or publisher—the knowledge claims in the paper are tenuous. However, it is possible for a journal article to begin life as an unpublished manuscript and then evolve into a paper suitable for formal publication.

*Professional Print Journals*

Because of the interdisciplinary nature of music therapy, articles can appear in journals in a wide variety of scholarly disciplines and health-related professions. For the purposes of this publication I would like to focus on those English language journals which publish music therapy articles predominantly.[2]

The American Music Therapy Association (AMTA) publishes the two most widely distributed journals devoted solely to music therapy. These are the *Journal of Music Therapy* (JMT) and *Music Therapy Perspectives* (MTP). Both publications are known throughout the world and are distributed internationally. Their large circulation suggests that they are the best way to reach a large audience, although a high percentage of the readers will be American music therapists. JMT seems to include research primarily but there is no mission statement in the body of the journal itself which attests to this. MTP is suitable for material with implications for music therapy practice. Its objective is to address the client service needs of practicing music therapists. In addition, the latter publication has a mentoring program

---

[2]And in the interest of full disclosure, I should mention that I am a member of the editorial board of the *Journal of Music Therapy* and the *Nordic Journal of Music Therapy*.

for prepublication which is oriented to providing assistance in developing articles for publications.

*The Arts in Psychotherapy* publishes articles in all of the creative arts therapies. As implied by its title, its focus is on psychotherapeutic applications, but this is not an exclusive focus. The articles in this publication tend to be theoretically sophisticated and its reading audience is large, very experienced, international, and multidisciplinary in nature. Five issues are published each year, many of which are theme-oriented around particular clinical issues. In recent years, these themes have included "Multiculturalism in the arts in psychotherapy," "Healing troubled communities through the arts," and "The body: Its politics, posture, and poetics." This journal is published by Elsevier Science, a publishing company.

The *British Journal of Music Therapy* (BJMT) is published jointly by the Association of Professional Music Therapists and the British Society for Music Therapy. Two issues are published annually in a wide variety of areas: research, theory, philosophy, assessment, case studies, history, and professional, political, and ethical issues. In addition to full-length articles, the journal also publishes miscellaneous shorter pieces that can include, but are not limited to, reactions to previous articles. There is a long history of music therapy in the U.K. and the size of the music therapy profession is probably second only to that of the United States. Articles in this journal will reach a large number of music therapists from a variety of theoretical orientations, although many will be interested in psychotherapeutic and related applications of music therapy.

The *Nordic Journal of Music Therapy* was formerly published in a variety of Scandinavian languages but is currently being published in English by Sogn and Fjordane College, Norway. It is an excellent journal with a variety of clinical, research, and theoretical articles. This journal has moved from a more provincial focus to becoming a real arena for professional dialogue and discussion around a number of important issues central to the practice and theory of music therapy throughout the world. There are many publication forms that include responses to articles and authors' responses to the responses. The reading audience is international in nature and the intellectual discourse is of the highest level. In many ways, it is the most progressive music therapy journal and is eminently suitable for articles on a wide variety of philosophical, theoretical, and methodological issues.

Other English-language journals that readers may be interested in include those published by the music therapy associations in Canada, Australia, and New Zealand.

*Professional Web-based Journals*

This brings us to consider the phenomenon of web-based journals, which combine some of the advantages of print journals and unpublished manuscripts. These types of journals are new to the music therapy profession. Because this is such a recent and potentially influential development, the information in this section may be the quickest to become outdated. Publishing in web-based journals is advantageous in a number of ways:

Length. Considerations regarding the size of publication can be flexible in these publications because they do not have to fit articles into a predetermined number of pages. Thus, articles that are either smaller or larger than is typical for print journals can be considered.

Supportive Audiovisual Materials. Because of their electronic basis, it is easier to include supportive materials such as audio recordings or color diagrams that are much more problematic in print-based journals. Electronic publications should be considered for published works reliant on these tools.

Dissemination. It is far easier and cheaper to disseminate information through the web than through print. Anyone in the world with Internet access can obtain such publications, a scope of dissemination that can never be matched by any type of print publication.

Timeliness. Because dissemination is so simple, it is easier to get information to large numbers of people quicker through web based publications. There are some disadvantages to this form of publication as well, although these may be mitigated once the form of publishing becomes more commonplace.

Dissemination. Although many of us take Internet access for granted, this is not a universal privilege. Web-based publications are unavailable to people without such access. The flip side of this is that anyone in the world with such access can easily obtain these publications.

Format. This is a speculative consideration. I know that I do not assimilate information on a computer screen in the same way that I do when reading printed matter. If I must do careful reading, such as when proofreading, I must print the publication in order to be able to fully absorb the concepts and read with meticulous attention. Information that is web based may be harder to assimilate and thus not absorbed as fully.

Permanence. Again, writing at the dawn of the electronic digital age, it is unclear how this means of distributing information affects us psychologically. I wonder about the ease of access and transient nature of web-based publications. Because it is so ephemeral, do we tend to not consider web-distributed information with the same degree of seriousness that we consider printed information? It may be that these considerations lead us to consciously or unconsciously dismiss web-based information as not having the permanence of ideas coming to us through printed publications.

It is essential for us to consciously become aware of and discuss with our colleagues the impact of web-based professional publications as they become more prevalent. For example, the inherent limitations of printed journals, e.g., limitations of size, expense in production, have the indirect effect of making editorial boards highly selective in what they agree to publish. What remains to be seen is the impact of the lessening of these factors upon the selectivity of electronic journal review boards. It may be that the ability to publish almost everything submitted causes these journals to have more lax standards. It is important for us to monitor the evolution of standards as the forms of publication change, especially in music therapy where the need for including recordings in publications makes web-based publishing such an attractive alternative. However, it is clear that this form of publication takes advantage of some of the aspects of unpublished manuscripts (such as the ease of dissemination) while combining with this some of the advantages of printed journals (peer review). As such, this may be the wave of the future. Here are three examples of web-based journals in music therapy. The information is current as of this writing (December, 2001) and is taken from the web sites of the respective publications.

*Voices: A World Forum for Music Therapy* is published by Sogn og Fjordane University College in affiliation with the *Nordic Journal of Music Therapy* and is the result of a joint collaboration with the World Federation of Music Therapy. It is located at www.voices.no and there is no charge for access to its contents. As a web-based publication, it has an international scope with editorial representatives from different continents and topics that reflect the diversity of music therapy practice. While there do not seem to be any types of publications which would be precluded from publication, the focus of the journal makes it particularly well suited to articles with political dimensions such as clinical work with refugees, the influence of local culture on music therapy practice such as the effect of local musical styles on music therapy practice, or an examination of the varying conceptions of therapy as it is embedded in different world views.

Here is the mission statement of the journal, which is included in order to help you determine if it is a suitable publication for a particular article of your own:

> *Voices* support[s] the discursive practices of music therapists around the world. . . . . This publication will encourage participation from every continent and will nurture the development of music therapy practice, theory, discussion and debate. Because culture has an important role in music and music therapy, we will encourage contributions that find their source in the cultural influences of each continental region. [*Voices*] seeks to nurture the profile of music therapy as a global enterprise that is inclusive and has a broad range of influences in the international arena. The journal is particularly interested in encouraging the growth of music therapy in developing countries and intends to foster an exchange between Western and Eastern as well as Northern and Southern approaches to the art and science of music therapy.

You can find detailed information on how to submit articles for publication at the web site.

In addition to existing as a traditionally published journal, the *Nordic Journal of Music Therapy* publishes an online version located at its website, www.hisf.no/njmt. The online version contains papers and book reviews that are not published elsewhere and also provides ongoing discussions on a variety of topics. At the time of this writing, these topics include 1) General Criteria for the Evaluation of Qualitative Research Articles, 2) IAP Revisited, and 3) The Origins of Music. The contributions are comprehensive in nature and tend to deal with the multiplicity of facets of complex topics. It is an invaluable resource for the conceptual advancement of music therapy.

Another electronic publication is *Music Therapy Today* which is located at the web site of the Institute for Music and Music Therapy at the University of Witten/Herdecke in Germany at www.musictherapyworld.net. While *Voices* clearly intends to be the online equivalent of a printed scholarly journal, *Music Therapy Today* appears to be put forward as an alternative to traditional journals. There is no editorial board referred to and information on the web site suggests that papers will be published without being formally subject to a process of peer review. In fact the publication is referred to on the site as a magazine. The intent appears to be to provide a place for budding authors to disseminate research and other writings in an expeditious way and to get responses to the material from colleagues. Material on the site indicates that readers of the journal have the opportunity to submit commentaries to the authors. The entire effort is put forward as a magnanimous gesture to support the elevation of presentations and writings in music therapy. Content areas include clinical practice, research showcase, and a teaching forum.

*Forms of Publication in Professional Journals*

Although scholarly articles comprise the primary content of most academic journals, there are a variety of other writing formats included in them such as responses to articles, essays, book reviews, and interviews. All of these forms provide essential scholarly functions that can be overlooked by potential authors wanting to make a contribution to the profession.

The focuses of scholarly articles generally fall within the areas of research, clinical work, theory, education and training, and ethical and other professional issues. In the area of research, most journals will publish qualitative, quantitative, historical, and philosophical studies as well as reviews of existing literature. While criteria for publishable articles can vary among different journals, a common requirement is that the article be an original work that makes a novel contribution to the professional literature.

Responses to published articles are an essential component of scholarly publishing that is too often neglected in the music therapy literature. Publishing responses in a timely manner—often in the issue following the original article—can greatly accelerate the conceptual advancement of a profession. Authors who respond to articles can offer differing viewpoints on matters of opinion, clarify and amplify the idea of the original article, expose fallacious conceptual foundations or inferences from the original article, or build on the original article to reveal implications that were not considered by the original author.

While all of these functions are important ones, typically they do not deal with concerns broad enough to warrant the publication of a new article. Hence, publishing responses to articles performs an essential scholarly function that cannot be accomplished in any other way. Two of the online publications above, *Voices* and the online version of the *Nordic Journal of Music Therapy*, are taking a lead in this area and both areas are including responses to specific articles. The *British Journal of Music Therapy* also does not seem to shy away from publishing article responses.

The *Nordic Journal* includes a variety of writing forms, in addition to articles, that go under the titles of "Essays" and "Clinical Perspectives." Such actions recognize that important scholarly contributions take a variety of forms. Essays allow for the exploration of topics in a more personal, individual, and fluid manner than would be suitable for a research study, and the exploration of clinical perspectives allows for the dissemination of information relevant to practicing music therapists, whether or not the information has resulted from the rigors of a formal research study.

Sound clinical applications of existing or new theory can be of great use to clinicians who make up the large majority of those who read professional journals. However, not all music therapy journals include publications in formats other than that of the traditional article. Hence, it is important to learn the culture of the various journals and to submit publications to the appropriate journal based upon the types of writing formats that they include or even solicit.

Book reviews are typically undertaken in one of three ways: a journal editor receives a book from a publisher and sends it out to be reviewed; an author provides copies to reviewers asking them to review the book for a particular journal; or the writer of a book review submits it unsolicited to a journal for publication. Individual custom seems to dictate which of these avenues to publication is taken.

Scholarly book reviews share some commonalities with the commercial review of books and films, but they go beyond this activity as well. One of the common functions is to help the reader of the review determine if the book is one that he or should purchase. Thus it is essential for the reviewer to describe the contents of the book, the intentions behind the book, and to offer substantiated opinion on the merits of the intentions and the extent to which these intentions were successfully fulfilled.

Some book reviews in scholarly journals stop at those points, but for certain books that address complex theory or that put forth novel or controversial positions, it is important for the reviewer to go further to include a more general discussion of the overall argument and perspective taken in a given book. This type of critical review deals not only with the book at face value, but also explores its conceptual underpinnings and the place of the ideas put forth in the book in relation to ongoing issues of general concern in the profession. This type of review puts the content of the book in a scholarly context so that readers will be in a better position to understand the issues it raises and can read it with more of a critical, scholarly frame of mind. The scholarly reviews of books have an obligation to include critical material and not just serve as publicity for the book.

Interviews also have a role to play in scholarly journals. A good interview is more than just a series of questions and answers but in addition conveys the sense of a dialogue between two people. The role of the two participants may differ somewhat as the agenda of the interviewer is to draw out the ideas of the interviewee, but this does not mean that the interview cannot be a dialogue of sorts. A dialogic interview can be very instructive as the interviewer plays the role of the reader, asking questions to clarify or elaborate upon the answers provided by the interviewee, or even disagreeing with the interviewee and seeing how the differing point of view is taken up. Because of their conversational structure, interviews are generally easier to read than are articles.

Recently published interviews illustrate two different ways of incorporating them into scholarly journals. The *Nordic Journal of Music Therapy* recently published a series of interviews—Forinash (2000), Bruscia (2000), Aigen (2001a), Amir (2001)—on the question of meaning in music therapy. Including interviews with four different practitioners ensured that the topic would be covered in a more comprehensive manner than would be the case with a single interview. All of these interviews were conducted by Brynjulf Stige and they illustrate how interviews can be a genuine dialogue, even though the majority of the content was provided by one person (the interviewee) as Stige's contributions take the form of elaborations or syntheses of the interviewee's comments with a request by Stige to respond to his reaction.

In a second type of interview, the questions have a less dialogic quality, instead functioning more to draw out a specific body of information and opinion from the interviewee. An example of this type of interview can be seen in Lisa Summer's interview of Helen Bonny (Bonny, 2001). This interview on music and spirituality was part of a special issue on "The Role of Music in the Music Therapy Process" in Volume 19(1) of *Music Therapy Perspectives*. Very often, this type of interview is appropriate when the interviewee is of a stature in the field where his or her ideas have inherent interest.

### *Book Chapters*

Chapters in edited books are usually done by invitation. Editors typically draw upon their own experience and search journals, conference books, and talk to other colleagues for ideas about potential contributors. Hence, your presentations and articles can lead to other opportunities for publishing. The level of editorial control and input varies among editors. Some provide a formal structure for all contributors to follow and others encourage authors to use their own judgment in putting a chapter together. In addition to the personal temperament of the individual editor, other considerations include whether or not the book is intended primarily as a text for use in universities. If so, there is more of tendency for the editor to request a uniformity of style and content in the book chapter.

*Monograph*

Although there is no formal determination for differentiating a monograph from a book, typical lengths seem to be anywhere from 30 to 90 pages. As a qualitative researcher, I find this to be a highly useful form of writing because its length allows for a singular focus more typical of articles, but with sufficient room for an in-depth exploration of a given topic. Publishers often make monographs available through a series which allows for the progressive exploration through time of a particular content area. For example, MMB Music, Inc. has a variety of monograph series, including the Horizon Series and the Nordoff-Robbins Music Therapy series. Because of its intermediate length, a monograph may also be a suitable length for publishing the outcome of an academic thesis or dissertation.

*Monograph Series*

At the time of this writing, a new publishing form in music therapy has been announced by Barcelona Publishers. This will be a monograph series in which each monograph will consist of several article-length reports of qualitative research studies. The series will be published on an irregular schedule that will be determined by the volume of submissions to it. Articles in the monographs will be subject to peer review, thus giving the publications greater scholarly weight.

All of the professional music therapy journals publish many types of research and they tend to place a great value on this diversity of approach. Yet this also limits the volume of published reports of any one type and also does not facilitate the type of advancement of the profession that occurs when particular publications are devoted to a more specific professional focus. The monograph series by Barcelona sets a precedent in music therapy publishing by highlighting the point that specificity of purpose in publishing has an important role to play. This is perhaps a more appropriate role to play by a private publisher than by a professional organization that has to meet a much broader mandate.

*Books*

There are a number of publishers who currently carry a fair number of music therapy titles. Some, like Barcelona Publishers, focus exclusively on music therapy; others, such as Jessica Kingsley Publishers, focus on a number of creative arts therapies; still others, such as MMB Music, include music therapy as part of a dedication to the field of music. Although conceiving of, executing, and getting a book published is an enormous task, this is an excellent time for publishing in music therapy. If you are interested in publishing a book, it is helpful to first get to know what type of book each publisher specializes in.

First, let us consider the idea of being the editor of a book with a variety of chapter authors. This is an enormous amount of work, but it can be very rewarding as it performs an essential service to the profession. In addition, it is not uncommon for editors to be contributors in their books, so editing a book may be one way of getting some of your ideas into print. It is also an excellent means to engage in a comprehensive exploration of a topic that you cannot cover alone. Some of the most important music therapy texts have been of this form, such as *Music in Therapy* edited by E. Thayer Gaston, 1968, and *Case Studies in Music Therapy* edited by Kenneth E. Bruscia, 1991. Barcelona has recently pioneered a number of important publications of this type: *Dynamics of Music Psychotherapy*, edited by Kenneth Bruscia (1998c); *Inside Music Therapy: Client Experiences*, edited by Julie Hibben (1999); and *Music Therapy Supervision*, edited by Michele Forinash (2001).

An expeditious way of putting an edited book together is to ask symposium contributors to prepare their addresses for publication such as in the publication *Music Therapy and Pediatric Pain*, edited by Joanne Loewy (1997). One caveat here is that the published versions of conference or symposia proceedings are more successful when they address an area of focus that is not well represented in the professional literature. As was mentioned previously, published information is more permanent than is presented information intended for immediate distribution and application. Hence, publishers may be less interested in a conference proceedings book unless it meets strict criteria of relevance and need in the profession.

Now let us consider what is involved in writing a book. This requires having a topic of broad enough interest to engage a large audience. Without this broad-based topic of general interest it will be difficult to convince a publisher to bring a book to publication. Certainly it is true that books oriented to academic music therapy training programs sell more than any other music therapy books and hence are most attractive to publishers. But the problem this creates is that the most attractive books to publishers are ones that are on the most basic level of theory and practice as they are oriented to music therapy students. However, as graduate training becomes more common in music therapy it is possible that specific course work in master's and doctoral programs will both require and generate more advanced materials.

There are a number of advanced texts being published in spite of the fact that they may not be of broad appeal. So it is clear that publishers will offer a wide variety of publications with varying levels of sales appeal, as long as the catalog in general is financially viable. The point here is that if you are interested in writing a book it is essential to be clear within yourself about the level of understanding the book is operating on and to which audience the book is being directed.

Different choices here include focusing on music therapy students, experienced professionals, a lay audience, or all of the above. It may seem odd to say that a single text could appeal to all these various audiences but a number of recent books in the literature show that it is possible to create books that do not presuppose a great deal of prior knowledge and yet can add substantially to the literature base and understanding in the field. Some examples are Colin Lee's (1996) *Music at the Edge: The Music Therapy Experiences of a Musician with AIDS*, Gary Ansdell's (1995) text *Music for Life: Aspects of Creative Music Therapy with Adult Clients*, Mercédès Pavlicevic's (1999) *Music Therapy: Intimate Notes*, and Julie Hibben's (1999) edited collection *Inside Music Therapy: Client Experiences.* All of these books have made important contributions to the music therapy literature while also being eminently readable by a general audience. This, of course, is another way of conceiving of a book that may make it more sellable to a publisher.

Regardless of the level of the targeted audience, writing a book requires in-depth and expert knowledge on the part of the author in a particular content area. Different types of content areas include a clinical approach, such as the present author's text, *Paths of Development in Nordoff-Robbins Music Therapy* (Aigen, 1998), a professional topic such as *Ethical Thinking in Music Therapy* (Dileo, 2000). or a particular theoretical or philosophical foundation for music therapy practice such as *Biomedical Foundations of Music Therapy* (Taylor, 1997). In developing an idea for a book it is essential to be able to clearly identify the area of music therapy that you are expert in and in which you believe you can make a substantial contribution.

This is not to say that you must know everything there is about a particular topic prior to writing a book about it. If this were the case no books would ever get written! Most (honest) authors will tell you that they learn a great deal in the writing of a book. So being expert in an area for the purposes of writing about it really means that you have enough knowledge to 1) articulate the scope of the book, 2) understand its relevance for music therapy, and 3) be able to seek out the relevant information and be able to evaluate it critically for its significance and relevance to your topic. In sum, although writing a book is an enormous learning experience, you must still have a very solid foundation of knowledge in the area prior to undertaking such a project.

A book can be an expansion or a distillation of a thesis or dissertation. Writing a doctoral dissertation does make us expert in a particular area. But often there are elements of a dissertation that are present to meet academic requirements that may not be necessary in a book. Method sections and literature reviews are such elements. This is not to say that just subtracting certain elements from a dissertation makes it work as a book. Often there needs to be a significant amount of rewriting done. But it is important to recognize that pursuing graduate degrees can be a path to writing a book. If this is one of your goals, then you may want to formulate a topic for the academic paper (dissertation or thesis) which meets the other criteria involved in getting a book published.

An excellent example to consider are the two publications by Carolyn B. Kenny (1987, 1989, respectively): *The Field of Play: A Theoretical Study of Music Therapy Process* was her doctoral dissertation and *The Field of Play: A Guide for the Theory and Practice of Music Therapy* is a book that emerged from the dissertation. The book contains a distilled version of the outcome of her research which involved an elaboration of the theoretical formulation presented to a multidisciplinary panel. Comparing these two works clearly illustrates the elements of a dissertation that can be omitted in a book. Generally, what is not included are explanations of research method, including illustrations of data analysis. The academic work focuses on the generation of research findings—in Kenny's case, the elaboration of an already existing theory—along with a detailed contextualization of the theory within a variety of intellectual traditions. In this work, the source of the ideas and their empirical validation are reviewed in detail. In the non-academic work, these elements are minimized if they are present at all, and the focus is on providing the theory in a more elaborated and creative fashion.

For potential authors or editors of books I would like to put in a plea to make sure that you include both author and subject indexes in it. Creating an index is a unique skill that few people are trained formally to do. With the advent of more rapid publishing turnarounds and the requirement of publishers for author/editors to provide camera-ready copy, the inclusion of a well-designed index is becoming scarcer in the professional music therapy literature. Again, there are numerous guides to compiling indexes; absent any other preference you may want to begin with the *Chicago Manual of Style* described previously.

It is absolutely essential to include an index in almost any book intended for a professional, scholarly audience. While some readers may read a book entirely upon first taking it up, many other readers read those portions that are directly related to their immediate concerns. An index can help these readers locate the relevant information. Moreover, even those readers who read a book to its finish often return to it time and again over the years seeking a quotation regarding a particular concept for their own publications. An index is an invaluable guide for a professional seeking all of the relevant material on a particular idea or issue in music therapy. The function of an index in scholarly books is as important as is that of a table of contents and its absence seriously limits its utility for researchers and authors and ensures that it will appear less in future citations than would otherwise be the case.

While most scholarly books whose primary purpose is conveying information require an index, there are a few types of books for which this is not always essential, such as reference books and books that focus on description as opposed to analysis or theory. For some books that function primarily as reference works, an index may be unnecessary if it would not contain information that was not available in a table of contents. Consider Cheryl Dileo Maranto's (1993) publication *Music Therapy: International Perspectives.* This book is primarily a compendium of music therapy practices, organizations, and training programs in 38 different countries and an index would not be warranted in such a publication. Another category of books is one that is directed both to music therapists and to general audiences where the focus is on description of processes rather than on acquiring scholarly detachment. Often the purpose behind these writings is to use a narrative form to tell a clinical story in order to convey the nature and significance of clinical music therapy processes. Two publications of this type are Hibben (1999) and Pavlicevic (1999).

CHAPTER 5

# Presenting

## General Considerations

We now move to a discussion of the live presentation of material, the other most common means of communicating with colleagues. I would like to consider what can be done live with an audience and the types of material better suited to this type of communication.

First, it is possible to share information in this format without many of the constraints that exist in writing. Topics and abstracts are reviewed by conference organizers, but because the entire content of the presentation is not reviewed, it is clear that the presenter has much more control over the content of the communication than does the author. Practically, this means that information for which it may be difficult to find an appropriate publishing venue can be more easily disseminated through live presentation. This can include information that is at a tentative stage of formulation, that is of interest to a relatively small audience, or that challenges orthodoxy in ways that make it difficult to disseminate. If the information you are communicating falls into these areas, presenting the information in conferences or symposia offers a viable, professionally sanctioned alternative.

Another reason to present material rather than publish it is the opportunity to provide materials—such as recordings—not always possible in conjunction with a publication. For example, some ideas—especially newer ones—require presentation together with the clinical material that provides the source of the ideas as well as their illustration. Live presentations afford the opportunity to present theories and other conceptual materials in conjunction with the clinical reality from which they spring.

In this way, as a presenter, you can do more than just present information: you can provide a vicarious experience in order to give the audience a glimpse of the experiential knowledge that informs your concepts. And at times we just want to create a vicarious experience for our audience, not just to offer some experiential knowledge to form the context for an idea but because we want our audience to know what it is like to have a particular experience for its own sake. Perhaps part of your focus is for the audience members to experience what music therapy clients experience so you engage them in a musical activity suitable for a therapy session. While your audience members are not becoming clients, they are experiencing what it is like to be a client in a session. Any communication that stems from having an empathic experience with what it means to be a client of music therapy is clearly better suited for a presentational forum than it is for a publication.

Presenting material at a conference allows you to hone your ideas through dialogue and to develop them further as preparation for publishing. Material that is not ready for publication can be made ready through the work you put into preparing it for presentation and the response that you get from interested colleagues.

Three of the largest venues for music therapy presentations are the World Congress of Music Therapy, held every three years with 2005 being the next one as of this writing; the national conference of the American Music Therapy Association, held annually in late October or November; and the European Music Therapy Congress, also held every three years with the next one scheduled to be held in 2004.

There is a difference between the European and American models of presenting and this difference should be taken into account in planning your presentation. Time allotments at conferences in the U.S. tend to be longer—typically 60–120 minutes—which makes the presentation a bona fide, in-depth learning experience. In the European model the time slots are significantly briefer—often 15–45 minutes—with the purpose of providing a basic sketch of ideas which are then pursued through publications or personal contacts. The European model provides breadth over depth with the idea that the more in-depth learning takes place outside of the conference structure. So as you plan your presentations, edit your material accordingly. For example, rather than thinking of a briefer presentation as a summary of a longer one, you may choose to focus on the specific elements that will engage your audience in a further exploration of your material, rather than on providing a comprehensive overview.

### Employing Clinical Materials

Although we will discuss the integration of clinical material with the written and spoken word in a subsequent section, I would like to make some general observations here. I recommend providing clinical examples whenever possible in presentations, whether the presentations are of a more clinical or more theoretical nature. In general, most presenters do not take the best advantage of session material, paying insufficient attention to the extent to which the practice of music therapy is an experiential medium.

Verbal descriptions of clinical interactions must suffice at times when other examples are not available. But it can be quite difficult to capture the experience of music in this way. These descriptions can be used when the structural, relational, or symbolic aspects of music are being highlighted. This is because the actual experiencing of the music is secondary in these instances where the nonmusical referents of the music are what is of most importance. However, the limitation here is that the audience is not given the means of making independent judgment on the presenter's interpretations.

At times it is actually preferable to use audiotape examples from sessions even if videotape is also available. The use of audio focuses an audience on a deeper experiencing of the music because there is less sensory information to absorb. It is possible to experience the music in greater depth and detail and to generate an empathic experiencing of the client.

Videotape examples are essential when visual information is being conveyed. At times, it is essential to note the client's facial expression, body movement, eye contact, or depth of involvement. These are qualities which can only be communicated visually. Also, in presenting group work it can be advantageous to use video recordings in order to be able to distinguish among the various musical contributions. Similarly, when the client and therapist are playing the same instrument, the use of video can help the audience to distinguish the musical contributions of each participant.

## Organizing a Presentation

In preparing a conference presentation it can be helpful to do a dry run in front of a trusted audience and get feedback on the style and content of the presentation. This can include a local college or university with a music therapy program, co-workers, or a local group of music therapists. This type of rehearsal helps to increase your familiarity with the material and gauge how well it holds together. It has been my experience that material that seemed essential and/or well integrated when examined on paper has often seemed less so when actually presented to an audience. I often find that I must supplement material with spontaneous comments and delete material while doing a presentation. So do make sure you have in your own mind the absolutely essential points to be covered. Remember, not all your material has equal weight and some is background material or of secondary interest. It is helpful to know ahead of time what you will leave out if time is short.

It is also important to balance what you need to offer with what an audience can take in. Anyone who presents has a need to share ideas and material with others: this serves our need to disseminate information and our audience's need to take in information. But at times we have to omit certain material because it may exceed the capacity of an audience to meaningfully absorb it. In planning a presentation always keep the focus in mind and only include that material which best communicates this. Avoid including material just because you have it or like it, however tempting this may be.

In putting a presentation together it is essential to have a rationale for the sequence of material. The better sequenced the material is, the more easily it will be grasped by audience members and the easier it will be to hold their attention. In a case study presentation there is a natural, chronological sequence. In other presentational forms we must create the rationale. In general, it is best to order the material in a way to gradually build understanding as subsequently presented information is dependent upon that which precedes it.

It is also helpful to include audio and visual aids to learning, something that can be done with increasing ease and sophistication as computers become more a part of our lives. These types of aids provide a brief respite from the "ocean of words" coming at people and they also allow time for assimilating concepts and experiences. Tables, models, and charts can assist understanding by providing a spatial or metaphoric representation of knowledge. Moreover, it is commonly known that presenting information through a variety of sensory modalities aids learning. Don't forget that as a presenter you are in a teaching role.

In creating a presentation it is important to provide the right amount of introductory and background information. In other words, get to the point! A frequent mistake made by presenters is to provide so much background information that the novel contribution that is the focus of their presentation is either presented in a hurried fashion or not presented at all. Time management problems are frequent among less experienced presenters and most people will stay with their sequence of material rather than skip to the more important parts when faced with a time shortage. While it is preferable to plan accurately, we can all run short of time and this is why I suggest knowing the material you can omit if time runs short.

It is important to know how much knowledge you can assume on the part of your audience. If you orient a presentation to an audience of experienced clinicians, and indicate so in your conference proposal, then there is no need to review basic or foundational information in your presentation. Of course there may be people in your audience who can benefit from that information, but the point is that information shared in a conference presentation should represent some advancement of knowledge over what is commonly known among professionals. It is not your obligation as a presenter to review knowledge that should be assumed at the expense of the unique information comprising your contribution.

I have also learned to be cautious about relying on interaction from an audience. If the success of your presentation is dependent upon audience contribution, discussion, or questions, you are putting its potential success in someone else's hands. Your presentation is not a paid rehearsal and most conference attendees sacrifice a lot to attend. The presenter's obligation is to make it worthwhile.

It is also important not to be too informal or conversational in presenting. You are the expert (for that moment) and it helps to present your material with confidence. You believe in the value of your material and ideas and you want others to take it seriously, value it, and give it deep consideration. Your presentation of it affects how it is perceived and ultimately judged by others. While it is important to reach out to an audience and actively work to engage them, it is important not to do this at the expense of minimizing the seriousness of your purpose.

In sum, conference presenting is a performance of sorts. You have an audience to engage. Your goal is to inspire, challenge, and stimulate them. I have found that a clear, relaxed, but authoritative presentation style is most helpful. Your enthusiasm for the material can be conveyed, but it must be justified by what you present. It is absolutely essential to *trust your material*. If it is emotionally moving or intellectually stimulating, let the audience be moved or stimulated by it but do not tell them that it is moving or interesting. This is their judgment to make and the most effective presenters allow their material to do their convincing for them.

## Presentation Formats

There are two choices in presenting: either to read a paper or speak from notes. Each style has its own inherent advantages and drawbacks which transcend our own individual preferences.

Speaking from notes has a few advantages. It allows for more direct eye contact with an audience and the conversational tone we use when speaking this way can be more appealing to listen to. It also allows for spontaneity, adding comments as ideas come to us. This can also be done when speaking from a prepared paper, although it can be awkward when an audience senses a presenter shifting back and forth between prepared text and spontaneous comments. However, speaking from notes makes better use of the opportunities of doing something live. The presentation can feel more like a real interaction and thus has the potential to have a significant impact upon the audience members.

The are two primary disadvantages of presenting from notes. First, you run the risk of omitting important points if your notes are not specific enough. When the notes take the form of a series of topics to address it is possible that not everything you want to say will get said. Second, speaking from notes requires the ability to form grammatical sentences from phrases and topics. This is not always as easy as it sounds. A fully written out paper can have a narrative flow, articulation, and organization that makes assimilating the material easier for an audience. When we speak from notes it is difficult to speak with the same ease and flow. In sum, speaking from notes is best suited to material with which you are very familiar or discussions of clinical techniques and practices that may not involve the complexity of a more theoretical presentation.

In compiling a presentation outline it is important to discover the level of detail that works for you. I recommend building the outline around the basic topics of discussion with the essential points you want to make listed under each topic. When I have discovered a phrase that captures what I want to say in a clear and unique way I make sure to include these phrases completely intact in the outline. It is also helpful to organize the outline spatially on your paper with indentations that reflect the hierarchy of the organization. In addition, use graphic tools such as bolds, underlines, and italics to emphasize your main points. Abbreviations are helpful in keeping the outline to a more manageable size and to a more easily read format. When you are including instructions or reminders to yourself in the outline, be sure to include these in a different font from the material to be shared with your audience. And last, make sure that the size of your font ensures ease of reading for you and that the spacing of the lines allows you to look at a page and see its main points without it appearing cluttered. Remember, at times you want to be able to have the paper at arm's length, such as when lecturing from a podium, and this may require a visual layout that is different from what is required when you are sitting at your desk preparing your outline.

When working within the precise time constraints of a conference presentation it can be quite advantageous to read a prepared paper. It is much easier to ensure that a given presentation fits within a particular presentation slot when that presentation is fully written out. Moreover, reading a paper guarantees that the material is delivered in a clear, grammatical fashion and that all the main points are covered. And last, a paper is closer in form to that of an article so it is much easier to transform a fully written out paper into an article for publication than it would be to do the same for presentation notes.

The disadvantages of reading a prepared paper are that it can be difficult to listen to, it creates a distance between the audience and the speaker, it is hard to incorporate spontaneous comments, and it does not make use of the informal possibilities of direct communication between a presenter and an audience. Because a presentation is a live meeting among people, reading a paper that could be presented equally well as a publication may defeat the purpose of a presentation. In general, reading a prepared paper is best suited to situations where you are presenting material with which you are less familiar or that is relatively more complex.

Some factors bear on the previous suggestions: The first consideration is the skill of the presenter. Some people are able to read a prepared paper in a way that it sounds spontaneous and alive, and others are able to speak from notes in a way that is so fluid that it sounds completely written out. Obviously, these individual considerations should be taken into account when creating your own presentation style. Also, at times the size of the audience can be an important factor. In relatively large groups there is little direct contact between audience and presenter anyway, so reading a prepared paper may be preferable, while in a small group it might appear unnecessarily formal. In a conference setting one does not usually know the size of the audience beforehand, yet it can be useful to ask the conference organizers the capacity of the room you are presenting in so that you can have some idea how many people you may be presenting to and then plan accordingly.

One last issue to discuss in planning a presentation is deciding upon the level of interaction with an audience. The usual type of interaction involves soliciting questions from an audience and the four choices are to take no questions at all, or to take questions before, during, or at the conclusion of a presentation. There is no one best choice here and you should use the format that best accomplishes your aims, given the relative advantages and disadvantages of each choice.

In taking questions at the outset of a presentation you can accomplish a few different things as a presenter. First, you can glean information which will affect your presentation by discerning the group needs, interests, and levels of understanding. However, you should only do this if you have questions in these areas and are willing to adapt the presentation based on the answers that you receive. If you feel that there are prevalent misconceptions about your topic—or if you feel that your material is taking an unconventional look at a particular topic—taking questions at the outset of a presentation can be an effective way of engaging audience members, dispelling them of misconceptions, and earning credibility in their eyes as you show a willingness to tackle difficult questions.

For example, I attended a presentation on hypnotherapy in which the presenter began by saying he would take four or five questions about people's preconceptions and resistance to the concept of hypnotherapy. Questions from the audience involved concerns such as the placing of false memories in participants, inducing involuntary behaviors, and the loss of control by hypnotherapy clients. The presenter dispelled these misconceptions at the outset of his presentation in order to ensure that the audience would hear what he had to say with more open minds. Moreover, if he was an experienced presenter he probably knew the types of questions that would come up and already knew how he would answer them. He might have accomplished the same thing without the use of audience questions just by addressing the common misconceptions. However, beginning a presentation in that way tends to appear defensive and is not the best mood to establish at the outset. Perhaps the audience members did not have these preconceptions and bringing them up would not have been necessary. By allowing the audience members to furnish the material at the outset, the presenter created a bond with them, engaged their attention, and got to the material that he needed to get to.

Taking questions during a presentation has a few advantages: it keeps an audience engaged as they become more active participants in the presentation; the presentation becomes a real interaction between you and your audience, thus taking advantage of the fact that a conference presentation is a face-to-face meeting of people; it helps to ensure that the audience members are grasping the material being presented as they can ask clarifying questions; it helps you gauge how well the material is being taken in; and, it gives people the opportunity to disagree with you and engage in debate. This last consideration is an important component of scholarly activities that serves to advance a profession and it is too often ignored in music therapy.

There are also potential disadvantages to taking questions during a presentation. This activity can be a distraction for you as a presenter. If the material that you are presenting is relatively new to you, it might be better to hold questions until the end. It can also take up much of your presentation time, preventing you from getting to all of your material. If your presentation is tightly formatted and there are no inessential elements in it, taking questions during the presentation may leave you with an incomplete presentation. Also, audience questions can pull you into material that will be addressed later in your presentation, thus disturbing the sequence of material. Or you can be drawn into unrelated or nonessential areas of focus because particular questions may not be relevant to the central focus of your presentation. In sum, taking questions during a presentation does have a few uses, yet unless you are very skilled in managing your audience—answering questions quickly, learning to deflect questions that are off the topic, and finding ways to graciously silence audience members who may be more interested in speaking than in asking a question—taking this choice may harm your presentation more than it helps it.

It is possible to take questions at the conclusion of a presentation. This is probably the most typical and traditional choice. The advantages here are that you can predetermine the amount of time devoted to question and answer. Also, by waiting until your material has been fully delivered, you can preempt questions that may have arisen during the presentation. Moreover, by waiting to the end of your presentation to interact with your audience, the interaction can occur on a more educated basis. The only disadvantages of taking questions at this time are that potentially interesting questions from material presented early on can be lost and you run the risk of losing audience focus along the way if the material being presented is difficult or unclear.

## Computer-Assisted Presentations

As we have been discussing, many professional and scholarly presentations involve more than just speaking in front of an audience. Typical visual and audio aids to learning include video recordings, still pictures, slides, charts and diagrams put on overhead projector transparencies, and audio recordings of music and music therapy sessions. There now exist computer programs—PowerPoint is a currently popular one—that are capable of storing and playing back all of these media while seamlessly integrating them into a lecture. The visual graphics for charts and tables are far superior to what can be accomplished with a marking pen and transparency sheet and the digital quality of the audio and video material is at a very high level.

It may be that the utilization of such programs will become commonplace in the coming years as professional audiences become accustomed to the quality of presentation that such tools allow. In that case, all presenters will be required to acquire a working knowledge of these programs and there are numerous publications already available to assist users of these programs. Although I have not used these programs, I have viewed a fair number of presentations that have utilized them and thus am able to offer some comments upon their current merits and drawbacks.

Some of the advantages are obvious: the high quality of audio and video they allow; the ability to bundle multimedia presentations in one device; the saving of time during a presentation when all of the media can be controlled from one location; and, putting all of the control in the presenter's hands if this is desired. They also allow for (relatively) immediate access to all visual and audio information so that recordings and slides can be easily skipped if need be, or returned to for a second viewing. The software also allows for the entire presentation to be automatically programmed in sequence, again a great aid for presenters.

Some of the drawbacks of these devices are not so obvious. A surprising one is that at times I have actually found the sophisticated graphics of such programs to be a distraction from the content of the presentation. Hence, users of the programs are cautioned to ensure that the presentation serves the content and does not overwhelm it, as audience members may find themselves admiring a nice graphic design rather than thinking about the presenter's material. Also, it is important to consider the risk in bundling all of one's presentation aids in a single device. The obvious danger is that if there is a problem with that one device, all of the visual and audio information becomes unavailable. An unexpected software or hardware problem could be devastating to a presentation where the audio and visual material was essential. Further, except for large-scale presentations such as plenary sessions or conference institutes, it is not common for conference organizers to provide the computers, monitors, or projectors needed when one uses such computer programs as presentation devices. Thus, presenters must supply, at the bare minimum, the computer to control the presentation and many presenters will not be able to secure the portable laptop computers typically used in such venues.

In sum, using computer programs as presentation aids has tremendous advantages, but there are some outstanding issues that may prove daunting to the infrequent or casual presenter. Those professionals with an interest in technology, a comfort level with computers, who value the aesthetics of presenting, and who plan to present on a regular basis are encouraged to explore these tools. Other professionals may want to wait until the equipment becomes more commonly available, or choose to use it only in those situations where there will be another person responsible for operating the presentation program who has expertise in that area.

CHAPTER 6

# Presentational Devices for Writing and Presenting

## Graphic Presentational Devices

Although graphic presentational devices perform different functions depending upon the type of presentation or publication they are serving, their primary purpose in a communication dealing with clinical, theoretical, research, or professional issues is to make a complex process or body of knowledge more intelligible and thus more easily assimilated.

Iconic or diagrammatic representations operate by increasing understanding through providing a metaphoric representation of process. The transfer of knowledge is mediated by the structural similarity between a process and its representation as we attribute qualities of what is known to that which is unknown. There are many examples of these types of devices in the music therapy literature, often illustrating different processes in music therapy practice.

Certain models illustrate client development. Consider Figures 1–3 from Robbins and Robbins (1991, pp. 58–59) study of self-communications in music therapy. Here the process of self-actualization through music therapy is modeled in the following way: In Figure 1 an irregular, amoeba-like shape represents the condition child that has developed in response to the limitations imposed by disability. An irregular boundary represents disparate levels of functioning in various areas. Figure 2 shows the music child—which exists at the center of the condition child—serving to extend the boundaries of the condition child, thus expanding the range of the child's functioning. Figure 3 illustrates the presence of the new self, an identity with broader and more well-rounded boundaries than possessed by the initial condition child.

In contrast, Carolyn Kenny (1989, colored plate facing p. 90) illustrates the seven overlapping fields (or elements) constituting the music therapy process as seven overlapping circles. There is a conceptual relationship among the fields that is reflected in the physical structure of the diagram, such as when the "musical space" is formed by the overlap between the circles representing the client's aesthetic and the therapist's aesthetic. The visual appearance of the circles also reflects their attributes: the open and expanding fields have porous visual boundaries and the closed fields have firmer boundaries. The overall beauty of the process is reflected in the aesthetic quality of the diagram itself. The power of Kenny's diagram illustrates the importance of consciously using all of the various graphic tools at our disposal.

Graphics can also be used to represent aspects of music that are not easily conveyed verbally. Carl Bergstrøm-Nielsen (1993) has developed a unique form of musical graphic notation patterned after graphic notation from unconventional forms of twentieth-century music and adapted specifically for use in notating music therapy improvisations. His approach involves the development of unique symbols to capture salient elements of improvisations. These symbols are mapped onto a graph-like structure where the horizontal dimension can represent time and the vertical dimension represents other parameters such as volume. These diagrams are used in various ways, including the discovery of important clinical themes and areas of countertransference. Thus, the diagrams have more than a representative function but can actually play a role in the clinical process itself. An excellent example of his work can be seen in the graphic representation of the first excerpt from the Nordoff and Robbins's "Edward" tape (Bergstrøm-Nielsen, 1993, pp. 54–55, Figure 5).

Charts and tables are traditional presentational tools that serve to organize information for presentation. The idea is that viewing the chart or table shows relationships among concepts or data in an easily comprehended form. A good table is more than a summary device, as conceptual relationships can be revealed that may not otherwise be obvious and questions can be answered in an immediate fashion. Thus, while viewing the chart or table can stimulate the thinking of one's audience, the process of creating the table can also serve to stimulate the author's/presenter's thinking to higher levels of conceptualization. Here are two examples:

First, consider Table 9 from Dorit Amir's (1991, p. 123) study of meaningful moments in music therapy. This table locates 15 categories of moments (divided into 2 groups: intrapersonal and interpersonal moments) on its vertical axis, while the study's participants (4 therapists and 4 clients) are located on its horizontal axis. A filled-in box in the resulting grid represents an individual who reported experiencing the type of moment in the row in which the box falls. Conveying the findings in this way allows the reader to make a variety of instantaneous comparisons, such as the relative prevalence of the different types of moments among all of the participants, the presence or absence of particular moments in clients as compared to therapists, and the types of moments therapists report regarding their own experiences as compared to their evaluation of their clients' experiences. In sum, this type of graphic representation allows for many types of analysis and allows the readers to ask their own questions of the data, some of which may not have even been thought of by the author. It allows for a deeper engagement with the text.

One other example is Table 1 from my own work (Aigen, 1993, p. 20). This table summarizes areas of congruence between qualitative research and creative music therapy practice and consists of three columns: qualitative research practices, music therapy practices, and a central column which labels the area of commonality the practices contain. Initially, I just created a list of practices and precepts from each domain that were similar to one another. This stimulated me to think about what it was that actually connected the practices. This area of commonality, summarized in the middle column, really was the heart of the matter and helped me to organize the article. For example, in certain forms of qualitative research, rather than using a questionnaire or statistical test, the researcher is the primary vehicle of data gathering and analysis. This concept is referred to as the "researcher as instrument." Similarly, in creative music therapy practice the therapist's self is recognized as an important agent of change in the client's process. I conceptualized the similarity in the phrase "centrality of the human agency." This highlighted the fact that both areas of activity place individual relationship and sensibility above the administering of objective methods and/or tests, thus providing greater insight into why qualitative research was an appropriate tool for investigating creative music therapy practice.

Table 10. Illustration of a Table Facilitating Conceptual Insight

Areas of Congruence between Qualitative Research and Music Therapy.

| **Qualitative Research** | **COMMON GROUND** | **Music Therapy** |
|---|---|---|
| Researcher as Instrument | Centrality of Human Agency | Therapist's Self as Change Agent |
| Participants, not Subjects | Equality, Mutuality of Process | Clients, not Patients |
| Researcher as Participant-Observer | Equality, Mutuality of Process | Active, Self-Disclosing Therapist |
| Transformational Impact on Researcher | Equality, Mutuality of Process | Transformational Impact on Therapist |
| Importance of Trust and Familiarity with Participants | Valuing Human Relationship | Importance of Trust and Safety with Clients |
| Stance of Researcher | Contribution of Practitioner's Unique Experience | Awareness of Countertransference |
| Decreased Focus on Generalizability | Valuing the Unique and Individual | Self-Actualization as Goal of Therapy |
| (1) Peer Debriefing (2) Support Group | Employing Multiple Perspectives to Ensure Integrity | Clinical Supervision |
| Flexible Approach to Method | Valuing Creativity and Interactive Process | Allowing Course of Therapy to Evolve |
| Lessened Focus on Sin-gular, Objective Reality | Honor Multiplicity of Constructed Realities | Respecting Client's Lived Experience |

## Verbal Presentational Devices

The traditional experimental report is a model for many professional communications. Some of the characteristics of this type of report are as follows: an impersonal writing voice without a sense of the person behind the report; the structure is a formal presentation of assertions, facts, and procedures; and, the presentation is said to be value-free. In contrast, the motivation behind my view of professional communications is strongly influenced by progressive forms of qualitative research that use a variety of narrative structures in communicating on different levels of human experience. Specific devices are chosen for their ability to both portray the field of study and to function in a persuasive manner in substantiating the researcher's inferences and interpretations.

Given the points made by Atkinson (1990) cited in the present text regarding the function of the neutral writing voice in traditional research, we can see that qualitative research reports—and the types of communications patterned after them—are not unique in paying attention to the rhetorical function of narrative structures. However, they may be unique in acknowledging the use of such devices.

It is possible to utilize a number of different narrative devices to enhance the power, clarity, and appeal of our professional communications. Many of these devices serve to compensate for the deficiencies of traditional academic reports in dealing with nonconceptual material and thus are oriented to communicating affective content, making individuals come alive for an audience, and talking about topics such as values which are usually not considered relevant to scholarly and professional activities. The various devices presented below are suitable for publications and for live presentations. And while they are all drawn from the literature on how to convey the findings of qualitative research studies, they are equally suitable for a variety of professional communications, whether or not they are the result of research activities.

### *Personal Context*

The idea of presenting the personal context of the presenter/author is drawn from qualitative research. The rationale is that all forms of scholarly and professional activity, e.g., research, clinical practice and theorizing, are affected by idiosyncratic factors relating to our biographies and personalities and admitting these personal factors into scholarly work requires that we speculate upon their impact. This should not be automatically a part of all communications but it can be very useful when understanding the personal context of the presenter/author is particularly relevant to the topic and focus of the communication.

Providing this material can serve to engage an audience, but there are two areas of caution here: First, it is important that the personal material provided not overshadow the material being presented. This will defeat the purpose of including the material which is, after all, to facilitate the understanding of the material you are presenting. Second, it is important not to engage in gratuitous self-revelation. Not all topics that we present on or write will be enhanced by the presentation of autobiographical material. And even when this material is suitable, we have to be careful not to provide too much or irrelevant material. This will certainly alienate an audience and impede the communication of our basic message.

In research, the personal context is presented to raise the researcher's awareness about the idiosyncratic factors so that they are less likely to act on an unconscious level. This enhances the trustworthiness of the research findings. In this regard, informing an audience about possible conflicts of interest—such as when researchers study their own clinical work—serves this same function. In other types of communications these factors are relevant to a lesser degree. Another important function relevant for all types of communications is that providing personal material can help a live or reading audience to identify with and internalize the author's/presenter's process in a vicarious manner. Putting an audience into your place can help them to engage with presented material (text or talk) in a way similar to how you engaged with the area of inquiry. Your audience is then in a position to be more strongly impacted and changed through the vicarious experience.

There are a number of elements that can be presented in the personal context for a given communication, some of which are more appropriate for a research presentation and others which are of general applicability. You should only utilize those that are necessary to enhance your message and facilitate a greater level of understanding in your audience.

*Presenter's/Author's Motivation.* This can include personal and professional motivations. Think back to the motivations for communicating with colleagues listed at the beginning of this publication. Discussing these motivations in the communication itself can engage audience members by providing the context of the inquiry and it can enhance the degree to which they can open themselves to the material and experiences that you would like to provide, especially when they can identify with your motivations.

*Prior Experiences.* At times we have experiences in life that shape our inquiries and professional activities and that affect their presentation. An example would be discussing a form of therapy that you have been a client in or discussing a music therapy procedure that you have had nonclinical experience with. For example, it can be interesting for an audience when a music therapist who has had a music career talks about the parallels between songwriting or improvisation in the clinical and nonclinical domains.

*Relationship to Participants.* Often when we present or write about clinical work we use our own work as therapists as examples. Our experiences and relationships with clients often motivate our professional activities and influence these activities. The types of clinical stories that go beyond the more traditional distanced relationships can be engaging and instructive.

*Potential Biases and/or Blind Spots.* Often we have prior experiences or prejudices that may distort the information we provide or render it complete. For example, are you writing about a music therapy group for individuals with eating disorders while having had experience with this condition in your family? Or did you have particularly salient countertransference issues that were motivated by a particular client? It is both intellectually honest and personally engaging to reveal this information in our professional communications, to the degree that is warranted by the purpose of the communication. The point is that while our motivations can serve our communications by strengthening our commitment to our work, they can also affect them in hidden ways.

In addition to providing audiences with important information, by including autobiographical factors in our professional communications we are giving each other the permission to better integrate our professional and personal lives. The more of our human capacities that we can bring to bear on our professional communications the more effective these communications will be and the more the profession of music therapy will be similarly advanced.

Here is an example of a portion of a researcher's context from a current publication of my own (Aigen, 2002, pp. 3–4). Although this is a research study, the same type of information could be provided in a clinically-based report that was not the result of research. Because the topic of the report—the improvisational use of popular styles in music therapy—was very close to my nonclinical musical identity, I realized that there were many autobiographical factors that influenced the research activity and I describe some of these in this brief excerpt:

Example 6. Illustration of a Personal Context from a Publication

---

The central focus of this study is the role of rock and related musical styles within clinical improvisation as revealed through the therapy process of a 27-year-old developmentally delayed man named Lloyd. The roles of the present author are multiple in this work functioning as co-therapist to Lloyd as well as the researcher and author of this document.

Of the various projects that I have engaged in as a music therapy researcher this is the most personal. The experiences I have had as a musician and listener in relation to rock, blues, and jazz music have directly influenced my decision to become a music therapist, my development as a clinician, and the way that my theoretical thinking has developed in a music-centered direction. Although I have always been aware of this connection, engaging in the clinical work presented herein, and attempting to understand and amplify its broader meanings through research, has made me much more aware of how extensively my experiences in music have affected my clinical practice and my basic understandings about music therapy.

I have been involved in personally significant musical relationships through improvisational rock music with a number of individuals, some of these in a band that I worked, lived and traveled with over a period of two years, and others have been with individuals that I have now been playing music with for the past 20 years, albeit in a less regular fashion. This experience of being part of a band—whether a literal one that also existed as commercial entity and was time-bound, or one that exists more in the beings of the members and which stretches across time and space—continues to be an alive and powerful one for me. What began as childhood fantasy has now continued into middle age as an important force in my life. Hence, I conclude that there are powerful, perennial, even archetypal forces that become activated in this way of being together in music.

In the study above, I discuss the clinical value of the communal feelings and experiences created when improvising in music that is based on groove. But I wanted to make it clear that some of these ideas had their source in my nonclinical experiences in music. I felt that it was important for my audience to have that information in order to assess the value of the theoretical ideas from musicology I was applying to music therapy. This is an example of providing personal information that is relevant to the topic and focus of a communication.

### *Constructs*

A construct is a narrative device written in the first person from the perspective of someone other than the author of the construct. Diane Garner (cited in Ely, Anzul, Friedman, Garner, and Steinmetz, 1991) defines a construct as "an inferred soliloquy based on the content of repeated observation and an interpretive composite of one [person's] . . . seemingly characteristic thought and behavior. The construct contains statements which are considered central to the way the [person] perceives his or her experience" (p. 153). A construct is a vehicle for clients and research participants to speak directly to professional audiences, albeit mediated through the sensibilities of authors, researchers, and presenters. Writing a construct requires that the author put him/herself in the position of the client participant and attempt to communicate the reality of the person being portrayed in the construct.

Constructs can serve a variety of functions. They are a way of communicating to an audience in a fuller way the nature of the clients and research participants that we write about. They can engage an audience's attention through making relatively dry clinical background material come alive. It also becomes easier for other professionals to apply presented ideas to their own clinical work as they can recognize similarities between the clients presented and their own clients. A construct is an excellent way of conveying the emotional reality of clients and research participants and at times this is of value in and of itself.

Because the process of writing a construct does require that we put ourselves in the position of our clients it is possible that we get useful clinical insights in this way. As an example, consider the following construct from a year-long study of a music therapy group (Aigen, 1997, p. 5). It portrays Brandon, an autistic adolescent prone to unpredictable physical and verbal outbursts:

Example 7. Illustration of a Construct

---

I like to hold Diane's hand. Andrew and Joey hug Diane sometimes. . . NO TOUCHING!! Keepyourhandstoyourself. Only when we dance can we touch. That's why I like the song "Swing Your Arms." I jump up and down in the music and touch Diane. Other times I stick my tongue out at her or touch her foot with mine when no one is looking. She moves away and screams. Want to buy some lamb chops?

Why won't she sit next to me? It's like in school and on the bus when no one wants to sit next to me.

Sometimes I feel like I'm going to explode. I can't hit other kids, and so I squeeeeeze my hands and JuMpUpJuMpUp and land BOOM! On the chair. No hitting! I try to get Diane to hit me. I want her to touch me.

The meaning that emerges from juxtaposing the last two statements of the construct was not something that I formulated prior to writing it. That there was a connection between Brandon's positive desire for physical contact and the negative way that he evokes aggressive acts from others only emerged as I wrote the construct. This is an example of how utilizing a presentational device can actually generate insights into our clinical work. The content of the construct reflects some quotations from the client in addition to my own inferences about his mental state and affect, drawn from researching the therapy group of which he was a member.

### *Themes*

As a vehicle for reporting the findings of qualitative research, Margot Ely (1984) defines a theme as "a statement of meaning that [runs] through all or most" of one's data or "one in the minority that carries heavy emotional or factual impact" (p. 6). Thus, the criterion for a theme can be quantitatively or qualitatively based. Themes function to summarize large volumes of research data but they are also an effective way of conveying other types of clinical information, whether or not it has emerged from a research report.

Themes are typically stated in the first-person voice of the individual whose experience the theme is representing. Themes can consist of verbatim quotes or alterations of quotes. Typically the alteration involves changing a statement in the second or third person to the first person, or expanding a statement with a specific referent into a more general form.

In the text *Being in Music: Foundations of Nordoff-Robbins Music Therapy* (Aigen, 1996). I presented the underlying philosophy of the Nordoff-Robbins approach primarily through a large set of themes divided into a number of categories. Here are two examples of verbatim quotes of Paul Nordoff from a training course for music therapists along with the themes derived from these quotations (among others).The first example is constructed by changing the voice from second person to first person. The second example illustrates how a theme is created by taking a specific statement and drawing it into a more generalized form.

Example 8. Illustrations of Themes

---

*Quotation*
Don't forget, you're communicating too. You can't base the session entirely on what the child is doing. You yourself are communicating, your communications are, or should be, certainly inspired by the child in the situation so they have meaning.

*Theme*
We can only help a child develop relatedness and communicativeness if we creatively offer them someone—ourselves—with whom to relate and communicate.

*Quotation*
He [the child] becomes an active partner in therapy. You'll not just pour in therapy to him like spoon-feeding a baby, no indeed! You are making it possible for the child, through his music child, to become a co-active therapist with you and together you create the therapy. Together the thing takes its form, its line of direction. Then the changes occur.

*Theme*
In the evolution of the course of therapy, we are equals with the children with whom we work. Often they are the teachers.

Themes can be effective in conveying the experience of classes of clients in music therapy. For example, if you wanted to present material on "Changes in Self-Image in Music Therapy with People with Eating Disorders," themes can effectively summarize the particulars of individuals' experiences into larger conceptual categories. They are also useful in conveying things such as values or belief systems because they are general abstractions which have specific beliefs and incidents as their source.

### *Critical Incidents*

Critical incidents are descriptions of actual occurrences that convey important meanings, central to our particular communication (Ely et al., 1991). Typically they can consist of verbal and musical interactions, as well as other behaviors in music therapy sessions. Usually they are presented in an unanalyzed and distilled form.

There are a number of reasons to present extensive descriptions of sessions. First, it can convey the reality of what one is studying, putting the audience in your position as the presenter/author. It can substitute for audio or video recordings when these are not available and you would like your audience to have some sense of the experiential basis of the ideas, theories, concepts, or techniques you are discussing. Also, at times "what happened" is an important part of the information you are conveying. This is especially true in areas of clinical work that have not been extensively written about in the professional literature. Moreover, if you are discussing processes or stages of therapy, critical incidents can serve as important markers for the process as they denote things such as turning points in the process, a period of dramatic development for the client, or a profound interaction shared by the participants. The present author's study (Aigen, 1997) containing the constructs discussed above also contains many examples of critical incidents.

### *Literary Forms: Poems, Plays, Stories*

The status of narrative throughout academia has been changing in recent years. Increasing numbers of people are recognizing that narrative represents an eminently human form of conveying and assimilating information. Qualitative researchers have been making extensive use of literary forms of writing once reserved for the literary arts. The use of these devices has a number of functions: to embody findings through dialogue rather than explaining them; to express the poetic truth of an area of study or human experience; to make a particular milieu come alive; and to present information and knowledge through presentational forms that will enhance its applicability. A recent text which focuses entirely on writing is *On Writing Qualitative Research: Living by Words* (Ely et al., 1997). Although it focuses on the use of narrative structures to convey qualitative research findings, it is equally relevant for all types of professional communications, whether or not they have resulted from research activities.

Diane Austin is a music therapist who has been presenting the results of her study of Alcoholics Anonymous through the form of a dramatic play and her work is represented in this text. She describes the structure and function of her play in the following way:

> The play is comprised of four composite characters. These characters give voice to what I learned about Alcoholics Anonymous. The main themes and my analysis of the data are presented in dramatic form. Most of the dialogue is taken directly from my field log. I consider this play, "Grace Street," to be the culmination my research. (personal communication, March 2001)

Included in the performance of the play are songs that reflect the feelings and general experience of the participants in her research.

If you have questions regarding the appropriateness of these literary forms in scholarly contexts, consider that the works that are considered to comprise "the substance of Western thought" (Cairns, 1961, p. xiii) are none other than Plato's dialogues. These dialogues are not philosophical treatises put forth in the form of conversations in a contrived manner, but are stories in the truest sense, containing much human drama. The dialogues allowed Plato to address the most profound of questions facing human beings, although in their use "he never subordinated meaning to form" (Cairns, 1961, p. xiv).

And this is an important consideration in using any of the narrative devices discussed in the present work. None of them should be employed in your publications in an automatic or casual manner. These devices are not ends in and of themselves and you should chose that device that best conveys the meanings that you want to put across. Otherwise you are putting the form of your message before its content. This will both obscure your message and produce a less than satisfying experience for your readers as they are left wondering why they are reading a poem or a play in a scholarly publication.

### *Layering*

Again, led by authors of qualitative research reports, scholarly and professional communications are increasingly making use of the phenomenon of layering. This is the intermingling of different voices, stances, epistemological positions, and sources of information in a single communication in order to create a more complete portrait of a phenomenon or milieu of study. Combining information from many perspectives contributes to this completeness of understanding and combining different types of information—such as objective observations, intuitive understandings, affective reactions, musical forms of knowledge—performs a similar function. Drawing information from a multitude of sources certainly serves to maintain audience interest while also facilitating the transferability of information that we all hope takes place as a result of our communications.

For example, in a clinically-based report there are many possible sources of information: session notes or transcripts; client reflections; observations from the therapist taking either a scholarly, clinical, or personal stance; objective descriptions of events; the observations of third parties, e.g, parents, caretakers, or other professionals; musical transcriptions; and other client productions such as poems or artwork produced as part of the therapy process. A well-layered clinical report can include many of these different types and sources of information. Again, I can refer to *Here We Are in Music* (Aigen, 1997) as an example of a report that was based on the concept of layering. The report comprised objective session descriptions of events (critical incidents), transcriptions of music improvised in the session, constructs introducing the group members to the readers, interviews with therapists, and my perspective as a researcher.

CHAPTER 7

# Media for Presenting Clinical Material

Clinical session material can be presented verbally, through audio recordings, and through video recordings. Previously, it was only possible to present recordings in live presentations, but rapid changes in the publishing and media worlds are opening up many other possibilities and they are changing the way that information is disseminated in the scholarly and professional domains. First, publishers are more willing to include compact disc recordings along with book publications, such as in the following publications: Ansdell, 1995; Lee, 1996; Aigen, 1998; Summer and Nolan, 2001; Nordoff and Robbins, 1977. Second, due to their relatively compact size and low cost, it is clear that DVDs will soon be included in publications as well. Third, the possibility of making available audio and/or video recordings through the Internet may allow an even easier way of making recordings available to readers. And last, it may be that computer-based publications—such as on a CD-ROM or other medium—will allow for the integration of text, audio, and video in ways that are just being foreseen. Although we are on the cusp of these momentous changes, it is true that we still have to work with the technology that is available to us today, and that is what I would like to discuss in the present section.[1]

## Verbal Presentation

At the outset I would like to emphasize the importance of presenting audio and/or video recordings of music therapy sessions in our professional communications. The intentional use of music and musical experiences to

---

[1] The material in this section is highly dependent on the current state of audio, video, and computing technology. Because change occurs so rapidly in these areas, all of the technical information presented here is subject to being superceded in a relatively brief time.

enhance the lives of clients defines music therapy. Being able to use the elements of music with clinical intent is one element of advanced clinical practice. For example, recordings of clinical music are essential to the practice of advanced specializations in music therapy such as the Nordoff-Robbins approach and Analytical Music Therapy. It is near to impossible to facilitate the advancement of the profession of music therapy without reference to the specific elements of music that come into play in clinical processes, and it is very difficult to adequately reference these musical elements without hearing them. When all we have is words to interact with, we wind up emphasizing aspects of music and aspects of music therapy work that are easily talked about, but which may not be central to the actual practice of music therapists.

Yet, it is not always feasible to include recordings of any type with our professional communications. In spite of the change in this area, most publications still do not include companion recordings and even in live presentations it is not always possible to obtain client permission for the use of session material for purposes of education, training, and research. Thus, at times all we have is verbal descriptions of clinical music therapy sessions and we should not ignore the fact that a wealth of information can be conveyed verbally. However, the verbal description is not a substitute for a musical recording but a translation of the music into another medium. And we should be aware that not all of the qualities of music can be translated equally well.

Some aspects of clinical music can be conveyed verbally (or visually). First, it is possible to represent clinical music through formal musical descriptions including traditional notation. This can include tonal and/or rhythmic information. While it can be very time consuming to transcribe music from clinical sessions, even brief notations of particular melodies, motifs, or rhythmic patterns can assist an audience in understanding the clinical music. Discussions of music in terms of its stylistic characteristics can also be helpful. When clients improvise music they are influenced by the music that they have heard all of their lives and their spontaneous expressions often have characteristics of different styles. For example, saying that a client tapped a cymbal in the dotted rhythm typical of swing music, or played a snare drum on beats two and four as is typical of rock music, helps the music to come alive for the audience.

In an improvisation it is also possible to discuss the quality of the client's music in terms of the dynamics of the musical interaction. Thus, a client's music can be described in terms such as complementary, leading, provocative, or inviting. The improvisation assessment profiles (IAPs) of Kenneth Bruscia (1987a) offer a multitude of possibilities in this area.

And last, it is also possible to report the therapist's impressions of the music in the form of feelings, images, intuitions, and narratives that come to mind. This can be effective in communicating some of the expressive qualities of the music or the clinical themes, when the music is considered as a symbolic expression. Mechtild Langenberg (Langenberg, Frommer, and Tress, 1993) has created an approach to qualitative research in music therapy that deliberately uses these latter types of reports to discern clinical themes.

## Audio Recordings

There are many choices of audio format for music therapists to record, archive, present, and disseminate their work, although it is clear that digital formats will soon predominate. There are a variety of reasons to provide audio recordings of music therapy sessions in our communications with colleagues. First, providing a direct experience of the music in a therapy session is a legitimate goal for its own sake. As music therapists we have verbally encoded explicit knowledge that guides our actions and we also have musical knowledge that cannot necessarily be transmitted verbally. This is not knowledge *about* music but *musical knowledge* which becomes instantiated in our musical actions. One of the ways that implicit learning can take place is through exposure to the musical interactions that comprise music therapy sessions. As we consciously internalize guidelines to practice we simultaneously take in musical forms of knowledge through recordings.

Providing examples of clinical music also serves to provide the basic data or information upon which our clinical interpretations and inferences are based. This is a double-edged sword for a presenter or author because while the recording can substantiate your interpretations it can also provide the grounds for these inferences to be challenged by your audience. While this may not be personally comfortable, the kind of dialogue that this can promote is an important step in our development as individuals and in the development of the profession.

The presence of clinical music also serves to ground the concepts and theories we present in actual clinical practice. Theories and concepts that are grounded in this way are more likely to be of use to other professionals. It also facilitates the understanding of the concepts to be able to experience their direct application through clinical recordings and thus they can be more easily applied by other practitioners.

Audio recordings have the advantage of engaging an audience while preserving the client's anonymity. Because music is an aural medium we get the most important information about a clinical interaction through sound. At times it is actually preferable to present an audio recording over a video recording as the visual information may distract our audience from what we want them to hear in the recording. It is just much easier to focus on information from one sensory medium at a time, so even in instances when you have a video recording, you may choose to use the audio portion only. In sum, it is essential to provide recordings of music therapy sessions in your communications if you believe in the uniqueness of musical experience and its irreducibility to words.

Now to some practical considerations as we discuss some of the different audio formats available.

Analog cassettes are still prevalent, although they really are the choice of last resort. They offer the lowest sound quality and this decays as successive generations of tape are copied. This format is very time consuming to copy and work with and it presents difficulties in presentations because it can be difficult to skip over or repeat excerpts quickly. In contrast to digital media, once a sequence of excerpts is set, it cannot be changed without making a new recording. The main advantage of this medium is that the equipment for its use is common and easy to use. If the only possibility for you to record sessions is on analog cassette I recommend that you transfer the excerpts, once chosen, to some form of digital medium, such as compact disc, for a presentation or lecture.

Digital audio tape (DAT) is a digital storage medium that uses tape. It offers excellent sound quality but it is meant more as a temporary medium of transfer rather than an archival medium upon which to store music indefinitely. This is because tapes can lose information (referred to as dropout) or become stretched or otherwise impaired. It is a poor choice for presenting because the playback equipment is rare and expensive. It does not allow for instant access of different points on the tape because the tape must be advanced or rewound. But one can place index points on a DAT so that the machine will automatically advance to a particular, predesignated place. At the time of this writing there is only one commercially available DAT Walkman-style recorder.

Minidiscs are a relatively new digital medium with many advantages such as excellent sound quality and ease of use. Small player/recorders are available at very affordable prices and combined with a quality condenser microphone these small recorders offer excellent fidelity in recording and playback. Two types of discs and recorders are available at the current time: regular minidiscs that offer 74 minutes of recording and minidiscs with compression technology (MDLP for "long play") which allows for 5 hours of recording on each disc. The discs are also reusable and existing material can be recorded over.

Minidiscs offer instant access to the various tracks, something that makes it very simple to skip or repeat excerpts in a presentation. Moreover, once the disc is recorded the order can be rearranged in any way that you desire. Because they have real-time displays, it is very easy to locate particular events in a session and to access them for future use. The availability of minidisc players at conferences is highly uncertain and you should not expect for this to be provided. Hence, you should either bring your own player along with an assortment of chords to allow it to be connected to an audio or public address system, or you should consider transferring your minidisc recordings to compact disc for the purpose of presenting them.

Currently, there are three different audio compact disc (CD) formats: CD-R, CD-RW, and SCD as well as data audio CDs which are computer based. CD-R stands for "recordable," CD-RW stands for "rewritable," and SCD stands for "super CD." The first two are more common and SCD has just come on the market as of this writing. SCD is only available on prerecorded CDs. While CD-Rs cannot be rerecorded once they are used, CD-RWs can be reused many times in a way similar to analog cassette tapes. However, CD-Rs are significantly less expensive and seem to be more universally accepted in compact disc players.

Recording sessions directly onto any form of CD is currently more complex than recording on a minidisc. CD recorders are of the component variety rather than of the miniature style and are more obvious in a session room. In addition, most do not have direct microphone inputs which means that microphones have to first go through an audio mixer and then into a line input in the CD recorder. However, while they are not yet particularly well suited for session recording they are the best choice for presenting and publishing. The playback equipment is universally available and easy to use. It offers the best sound quality and most of the searching and skipping track features that make digital media so attractive. The best combination at the present for most users would be to record sessions on minidisc while converting these recordings to CD for use in publications and presentations.

One last means of making audio recordings available is through the Internet. The *Nordic Journal of Music Therapy* is currently publishing articles while making the sound file available at their website to be downloaded. This seems to make great use of the possibilities of the Internet by making available audio recordings to music therapists throughout the world without having to physically distribute the recordings. Of course this brings up very important questions of access and client confidentiality which must be addressed in the future as clinical materials become distributed throughout the world.

## Video Recordings

Many of the reasons for incorporating audiotape examples of clinical work in professional communications apply to videotape as well. What I would like to discuss here are the specific reasons to use videotape when it is available. Sometimes clinical work is oriented toward facilitating changes in what clients are capable of doing. But equally important is clinical work which is oriented to expanding the range of human experiences that clients can participate in. When clients are unable to engage in self-report, these types of changes are most evident visually by observing breathing, eye contact, facial expressions, and body posture. It is particularly important to be able to show these things when they are the basis for claims of clinical progress. Also, when motor skills and expression lag behind musical sensitivity, growth is better seen in the client's musical intent and degree of engagement rather than in the rhythmic or tonal precision of the playing. Again, this type of engagement is often best revealed visually.

At times, using audio recordings alone can focus too much on what is *not* present musically, rather than what *is* present. When audiotape is listened to there may more of a tendency to evaluate what we are hearing based on aesthetic or other criteria that may not be the most important consideration in a given course of therapy. For example, in a study on the use of popular styles (Aigen, 2001b) I discussed that a particular client was showing significant musical and interpersonal growth as evidenced by the sustained and focused nature of his cymbal playing in jazz-styled improvisations. In listening to the audio recording alone, the imprecision in the placement of his cymbal taps becomes more prominent compared to when the same excerpt is viewed on video. Focusing too much on the imprecision obscures the salient parts of this particular client's development. This is an example of where videotape is the appropriate vehicle for illustrating the client's growth because focusing solely on the audio obscures his degree of engagement and expression.

Practically speaking, at times the client's musical contribution is most easily discerned by having visual information available as well as sound. This is the case when the client's expression is too soft to be heard clearly, when the client is playing the same instrument as the therapist, or in a group setting when the various musical contributions can be difficult to discern. It is also important to consider that one's physical relationship to one's instrument is part of the music. Stravinsky has said that "the sight of the gestures and movements of the various parts of the body producing the music is fundamentally necessary if it is to be grasped in all its fullness" (Meyer, cited in Keil,1994, pp. 56–57). And at times musical sensitivity is apparent in one's physical relationship to instruments, such as the way one holds or strums a guitar, arches one fingers on a piano keyboard, or plays a drum with a fluid arm motion. This is especially important when these sensitivities are dramatically different from other areas of functioning.

One final consideration in evaluating the specific functions of clinical videotapes is that the best way to evaluate explanatory constructs is to have as close an experience as is possible to that in the session. The vicarious experience afforded to us through videotape is an important factor as we engage in the scholarly judgment of assessing the utility and appropriateness of the constructs put forth to explain music therapy process.

As we move into a discussion of the more practical aspects of using videotape, it is again important to state that changes in this area are occurring so rapidly that all of the technical information should be verified.

As of this writing, there are currently three different analog videotape formats with two of the formats available in a higher quality version. The most common videotape remains the ½-inch VHS format. This is the format that most of us are familiar with. Its primary advantages are excellent audio quality with most recorders and players operating in stereo, and the easy availability of equipment to play these tapes. Super VHS (SVHS) tape recorders offer a higher quality picture, a consideration that becomes especially important when you are making excerpt or compilation tapes. This is because the SVHS format allows for more specific color, contrast, and brightness adjustments when copying tapes. SVHS video recorders only cost marginally more than standard VHS recorders but SVHS tapes cannot be played in VHS machines. A good solution is to tape sessions in the SVHS format and then produce VHS copies of tapes to be used in conference presentations.

VHS-C tapes operate in camcorders much smaller than those available for VHS or SVHS recordings and this is their primary advantage. Their primary drawback is that most models operate in mono only and the tape lengths are shorter than are VHS and SVHS tapes. With the use of an adapter case, VHS-C tapes will play in normal VHS players.

Another analog video format is eight millimeter (8 mm) video which is also available in a Hi-8 format that is the equivalent of SVHS. The camcorders combine the small size of the VHS-C recorders with the higher audio quality and longer tape lengths of VHS tapes. The primary drawback of this format is that these tapes will not play in VHS players, thus necessitating that the tape be converted for use in most venues. Eight millimeter video players are extremely rare although the cameras are common and can be used for playback, although they tend not to be convenient for this purpose.

Because they are just becoming available, I will only make passing mention of digital video recording formats. These include digital tape formats such as DVC-CAM and DVC-PRO and disc formats such as digital video discs (DVD).The digital format in video has many of the same advantages over analog formats that are true in the audio domain. These include higher audio and video quality, better storage possibilities, ease of use, and ease of editing.

At the time of this writing, the various digital tape mediums are being used primarily for shooting initial footage and for editing purposes. The tapes are very expensive, the players are not commonly available, and there are multiple formats being used that are not compatible with one another. For these reasons, digital tape formats will probably not be of use to professionals planning presentations in the immediate future.

While the players are becoming quite common, the first DVD recorders have just come on the market as of this writing. These recorders are available in computer drives and as stand-alone components. The recorders offer a practical alternative to presenting work at conferences on analog videotape. One limitation is that the current generation of DVD burners do not produce DVDs that can be used for replication purposes. Hence, they are useful in producing single discs for viewing, but are not suitable to produce master DVDs that can be used to duplicate DVDs for training films, for example.

CD-ROMs are another digital medium that can integrate text, audio, and video, but at this time the video quality does not yet approach the quality of any of the other media.

CHAPTER 8

# Describing Clinical Material

There are many different situations in which clinical material is presented visually or aurally and each one requires a different approach to the type and volume of verbal description that best accompanies the material. One thing that they all have in common, however, is that they serve to direct the audience to those events in the particular clinical excerpt that represent your reason for using it.

In any recording, video or audio, there are a multitude of musical and interactional events. When we are familiar with a particular recording of our own clinical work we tend to see the important events in relief as the other information recedes into the background. It can be difficult for us to experience the excerpt as our audience would. But it is absolutely important to highlight the particular events on the recording so that we can be more confident that our audience will hear and/or see those events. And at times it is not a particular event or series of events that we intend to highlight but the overall musical, interpersonal, or expressive mood. Again, it is important to describe these musical and expressive qualities in a language that captures its essence and presents it for the consideration of our audience.

## Audio Recordings

I will first discuss some considerations when audio recordings are presented in conjunction with publications. Time-based description can be very helpful to readers/listeners. This can entail presenting a list of the salient events of the session along with the time on the recording that the events occur. This allows the audience to better hear the events referred to in the verbal description of the excerpt. When excerpts are presented through digital media these descriptions are especially useful as they allow the listener to follow the description as the excerpt is being played and to return to particularly salient events. Because it can be read while the excerpt is being listened to, the written descriptions of audio excerpts can be lengthy, complex, and detailed when appropriate.

Depending upon the function of the particular excerpt, a number of things may be pointed out to the reader. It can be helpful to begin by setting the scene for the reader in describing the physical location where the recordings took place. Providing this level of detail, while not necessarily important from a clinical standpoint, can perform an important function in helping the reader to feel the vitality and aliveness of the recording.

An important class of information consists of those factors not available because the recording is in audio. This can include client facial expressions, body movements and postures, and eye contact. These factors are particularly relevant when they represent salient aspects of the client's growth and clinical process. It is also important to clarify possible ambiguities for the reader, such as when client and therapist are playing the same instrument. Making reference to the register of the instrument or rhythmic pattern of the playing can help the reader to differentiate the client's and therapist's playing from each other.

In this vein, it can also be important to provide a level of musical detail in the description. This is particularly important when the recording is improvisational in nature. Items to include here include tonality(ies) of the improvisation, harmonic structures, rhythmic patterns, and transcriptions of melodies or motifs. One reason to include this information is that at times client development is reflected in these musical structures. If, for example, you are presenting work with an autistic child who improvises at the piano, and growth was seen in the coherence or complexity of melodies created, it can be important to demonstrate these claims through musical transcriptions. Certainly this information is available to readers to obtain on their own, yet you strengthen your points by substantiating them with musical notation illustrations that complement the verbal description and the recording.

Musical descriptions also enrich clinical descriptions because they provide insight into therapist's clinical interventions. A musical intervention on the therapist's part has many dimensions and possible rationales. One of the most important of these is that particular tonal, melodic, harmonic, rhythmic, and timbral elements have essential qualities that affect clients in particular ways. In order to fully know the nature of a clinical-musical intervention, and thus understand its significance, it is essential to be aware of what it consists of musically.

One final reason to provide musical descriptions is that they concretize therapist strategies and client-therapist interactions in musical specifics.

When we want to claim that a client's musical expressions represent clinical growth—such as when they manifest increasing complexity, responsiveness, or interactivity— it is important to substantiate such claims with a transcription of musical interactions that demonstrate the claims in musical terms.

Here is an example of the written description provided for an audiotape clinical example from *Music Therapy Perspectives* (Aigen, 2001b, p. 37) that illustrates some of the points we have been considering. It is taken from a study of a developmentally-delayed young man named Lloyd who worked in primarily an improvisational way through popular idioms:

Example 9. Illustration of a Time-Based Description for an Audio Clinical Excerpt

---

**CD Track 2** Index (:50)

:00 - Lloyd starts playing vigorously on the tom-tom drum in eighth-notes. The therapist responds by providing a rock pattern in the bass end of the piano.

:07 - Lloyd changes to the snare drum and then the cymbal in attempts to maintain rhythmic stability.

:18 - Lloyd finds this stability on the bass drum and maintains a series of eighth-note beats on the bass drum for almost 14 complete measures (counting in 2/4) at a tempo of 240 bpm (mm 120).

:22 - After vamping on the I chord, the therapist moves to the IV chord to establish a 12-bar blues form.

:26 - Lloyd adds the cymbal to his bass drum playing and then plays the cymbal alone.

:36 - On the turnaround of the 12-bar form, Lloyd changes back to the tom-tom drum in synchrony with piano and bass moving to the V7 chord.

:42 - Lloyd sustains the playing on the turnaround through the return to the I chord.

By describing the rhythmic structure of the client's playing (in eighth-notes) the point is made that his expression is musically organized. It also helps to explain why the therapist makes a particular stylistic choice as the eighth-notes on the cymbal are contextualized in a rock and roll feel. By explaining the client's intention (searching for stability) his rapid changes in instruments are explained. Because previously in the article the point was made that Lloyd only participated in sustained musical interactions for brief periods of time, providing the actual number of measures he plays in tempo highlights an important part of his development. Similarly, providing the tempo of his playing also attests to his development as it is more difficult for him to coordinate his expression at this fast tempo. And by noting Lloyd's change in instrument at a significant moment in the form (at the turnaround) it is implied that Lloyd is communicating his awareness of aspects of the form. In sum, this description enhances what is gleaned from listening to the audio excerpt by bringing attention to the salient clinical events.

When audio examples are presented in conjunction with the spoken word, such as in a conference presentation, the description must be more cursory than is the case with publications. Audience members cannot hold long descriptions in their mind while hearing the excerpt. So a detailed foreshadowing of the events will often be wasted. While it is possible to mention at the most two or three specific events that will occur on the recording, in general it is more useful to make general observations that reflect the purpose behind the playing of the particular excerpt. If, for example, you are playing a particular excerpt because it reflects the client's taking of initiative in the music, mention this fact and perhaps one or two specific examples. What you want to do in an oral description of an excerpt is to highlight the general clinical themes that the excerpt illustrates. Much of the musical detail that is essential in written descriptions can be lost in a spoken description. It should be offered in a judicious way, and only if it is vital to conveying the significance of the excerpt.

If you believe that it is vital to provide greater detail there are a few other options. You can speak over the recording as it is playing, bringing the volume to a lower level while you make specific points. This is difficult to manage well and is done better when there is a second person assisting you. You also have the option of providing detailed information on an overhead or on a handout. And last, it is also possible to introduce new information after the excerpt has been played. Some presenters prefer this option as they would like their audience to have a purer experience of the music, unimpeded by the concepts they are presenting. My own view is that presenting the conceptual information first is generally more helpful because it facilitates the audience's ability to focus on the more important aspects of the excerpt.

There are a number of publications in music therapy that have companion audio recordings and readers are directed to the following ones that illustrate different ways of using words in conjunction with music: Aigen, 1998; Ansdell, 1995; Lee, 1996; Nordoff and Robbins, 1977; Ritholz and Turry, 1994; Soshensky, 2001.

**Video Recordings**

When using video recordings, either live or in conjunction with a publication, words serve a different function from when they are used with audio recordings. Words set the context, providing the information needed to understand the significance of the excerpt. They can function to direct the audience's attention to the events of interest but the words need not tell in detail what happens because that is the purpose of the video.

Consider the following narrative description of the same clinical excerpt from Example 9 above which was utilized at a conference presentation:

> Example 10. A Narrative Description of a Videotape Clinical Excerpt
>
> ---
>
> In the following excerpt the primary therapist is playing rock and roll to Lloyd's vigorous drumming and the co-therapist is playing the bass guitar. On several occasions Lloyd is able to sustain his playing in the tempo of the music, especially on the bass drum which is played with a foot pedal. In fact, Lloyd was first able to play in a consistent tempo with the bass drum—had we not offered him this opportunity, we may have never known of his ability in this area. Through these consistent eighth-notes, Lloyd is able to connect musically with both therapists and participate in creating the rock feeling. Clinically, we can see how the rock and roll style both expressed and contained Lloyd's excitement.

Here, most of the musical detail is omitted because it will be difficult to remember, and descriptions of the client's actions (changing instruments) are omitted because it is apparent on the video. Instead of providing detailed descriptions of the music and the client's actions, the description serves to highlight the clinical significance of the excerpt in general terms, focusing on the way that the client is able to sustain his effort and the corresponding interpersonal connection that this affords to him.

When preparing clinical excerpts it is important to edit carefully, including only that material necessary to illustrate your main points. Choose beginnings and endings carefully, paying special attention to maintaining the musical integrity of the excerpt. For example, try to end the excerpt on a resolved chord rather than a suspended one, or allow the excerpt to end at the completion of a musical phrase rather than in the middle of one. Editing your excerpts in this way demonstrates a reverence and respect for the music itself as well as for the clients who produced the music. And always be clear in your mind on the significance of the excerpt and why you are using it. Important criteria in choosing clinical excerpts are that it represents a nodal point in therapy, it best exemplifies an idea or concept, it shows typical work, or that it is profound or emotionally moving.

# Afterword

Colleagues who read our publications and who attend our presentations are giving us something very precious: their time. It is important that we honor the privilege afforded to us by infusing our work with all of the intelligence and inspiration that we can summon. Different people look for different things from their contact with colleagues: some look for inspiration; others are more interested in information; and most of us desire a sense of communing with others who are engaged in a similar work that can be lonely and difficult at times. My parting wish is that you determine what it is you have to offer others and that you find the way to present it clearly, forcefully, and artistically.

# References


Achtert, W. S., & Gibaldi, J. (1985). *The MLA style manual.* New York: Modern Language Association.

Aigen, K. (1990). Echoes of silence. *Music Therapy, 9*(1), 44–61.

Aigen, K. (1993). The music therapist as qualitative researcher. *Music Therapy, 12*(1), 16–39.

Aigen, K. (1995a). Cognitive and affective processes activated in music therapy: A model for contemporary Nordoff-Robbins practice. *Music Therapy, 13*(1), 13–46.

Aigen, K. (1995b). Principles of qualitative research. In Barbara H. Wheeler (Ed.), *Research in music therapy* (pp. 283–311). Gilsum, NH: Barcelona Publishers.

Aigen, K. (1996). *Being in music: Foundations of Nordoff-Robbins music therapy.* Nordoff-Robbins Music Therapy Monograph Series #1. St. Louis, MO: MMB Music, Inc.

Aigen, K. (1997). *Here we are in music: One year with an adolescent, creative music therapy group.* Nordoff-Robbins Music Therapy Monograph Series #2. St. Louis, MO: MMB Music.

Aigen, K. (1998). *Paths of development in Nordoff-Robbins music therapy.* Gilsum, NH: Barcelona Publishers.

Aigen, K. (2001a). Music, meaning, and experience as therapy. *Nordic Journal of Music Therapy, 10*(1), 86–99.

Aigen, K. (2001b). Popular musical styles in Nordoff-Robbins clinical improvisation. *Music Therapy Perspectives, 19*(1), 31–44.

Aigen, K. (2002). *Playin' in the band: A qualitative study of popular music styles as clinical improvisation.* Nordoff-Robbins Center for Music Therapy at New York University (with video recording).

Aldridge, D. (1999). Personal opinion: Developing a community of inquiry. *Nordic Journal of Music Therapy, 8*(1), pp. 25–35.

American Music Therapy Association. (2001). AMTA code of ethics. In *AMTA member sourcebook.* Silver Spring, MD: Author.

American Psychological Association. (2001). *Publication manual of the American Psychological Association* (5th ed.). Washington, DC: Author.

Amir, D. (1991). Awakening and expanding the self: Meaningful moments in the music therapy process as experienced and described by music therapists and music therapy clients. Unpublished doctoral dissertation, New York University.

Amir, D. (2001). Layers of meaning. *Nordic Journal of Music Therapy, 10* (2), 209–220.

Ansdell, G. (1995). *Music for life. Aspects of creative music therapy with adult clients.* London: Jessica Kingsley Publishers.

Ansdell, G. (1999). Music therapy as discourse & discipline: A study of 'music therapist's dilemma.' Unpublished doctoral dissertation, City University (London).

Ansdell, G., & Pavlicevic, M. (2001). *Beginning research in the arts therapies: A practical guide.* London and Philadelphia: Jessica Kingsley Publishers.

Atkinson, P. (1990). *The ethnographic imagination: Textual constructions of reality.* Newbury Park, CA: Sage Publications.

Atkinson, P. (1992). *Understanding ethnographic texts.* Newbury Park, CA: Sage Publications.

Bergstrøm-Nielsen, C. (1993). Graphic notation as a tool in describing and analyzing music therapy improvisations. *Music Therapy, 12*(1), 40–58.

Bonny, H. (2001). Music and spirituality. *Music Therapy Perspectives, 19*(1), 59–62.

Bruscia, K. E. (1987a). *Improvisational models of music therapy.* Springfield, IL: Charles C. Thomas Publishers.

Bruscia, K. E. (1987b). *Perspectives on music therapy education and training.* Philadelphia: Temple University.

Bruscia, K. E. (Ed). (1991). *Case studies in music therapy.* Gilsum, NH: Barcelona Publishers.

Bruscia, K. E. (1995a). Modes of consciousness in guided imagery and music (GIM): A therapist's experience of the guiding process. In Carolyn B. Kenny (Ed.), *Listening, playing, creating: Essays on the power of sound* (pp. 165–197). Albany: State University of New York Press.

Bruscia, K. E. (1995b). Topics and questions in quantitative research. In Barbara L. Wheeler (Ed.), *Music therapy research: Quantitative and qualitative perspectives* (pp. 119–127). Phoenixville, PA: Barcelona Publishers.

Bruscia, K. E. (1998a). *Defining music therapy, 2nd edition*. Gilsum, NH: Barcelona Publishers.

Bruscia, K. E. (1998b).Techniques for uncovering and working with countertransference. In Kenneth E. Bruscia (Ed.), *The dynamics of music psychotherapy* (pp. 93–120). Gilsum, NH: Barcelona Publishers.

Bruscia, K. E. (Ed.). (1998c). *The dynamics of music psychotherapy*. Gilsum, NH: Barcelona Publishers.

Bruscia, K. (2000). The nature of meaning in music therapy. *Nordic Journal of Music Therapy, 9*(2).

Cairns, H. (1961). Introduction. In Edith Hamilton & Huntington Cairns (Eds.), *Plato: The collected dialogues* (pp. xiii–xv). Princeton University Press.

Dileo, C. (2000). *Ethical thinking in music therapy*. Cherry Hill, NJ: Jeffrey Books.

Ely, M. (1984). *Beating the odds: An ethnographic interview study of young adults from the culture of poverty*. Paper presented at the Seventh Annual Conference on English Education, New York University, New York.

Ely, M., Anzul, M., Friedman, T., Garner, D., & Steinmetz, A. M. (1991). *Circles within circles: Doing qualitative research*. London: The Falmer Press.

Ely, M., Vinz, R., Downing, M., & Anzul, M. (1997). *On writing qualitative research: Living by words*. London and Washington, D.C.: The Falmer Press.

Forinash, M. (2000). "I have to wait for the moment that I'm doing the music to figure out what the meaning is." *Nordic Journal of Music Therapy, 9*(1).

Forinash, M. (Ed.). (2001). *Music therapy supervision*. Gilsum, NH: Barcelona Publishers.

Gaston, E. T. (Ed.). (1968). *Music in therapy*. New York: Macmillan.

Hibben, J. (1999). *Inside music therapy: Client experiences*. Gilsum, NH: Barcelona Publishers.

Keil, C. (1994). Motion and feeling through music. In (Charles Keil & Steven Feld) *Music grooves* (pp. 53–76). University of Chicago Press.

Keil, C., & Feld, S. (1994). *Music grooves*. Chicago and London: University of Chicago Press.

Kenny, C. B. (1987). *The field of play. A theoretical study of music therapy process*. Unpublished doctoral dissertation, The Fielding Institute.

Kenny, C. B. (1989). *The field of play: A guide for the theory and practice of music therapy.* Atascadero, CA: Ridgeview Publishing Co.

Langenberg, M., Frommer, J., & Tress, W. (1993). A qualitative research approach to analytical music therapy. *Music Therapy, 12*(1), 59–84.

Lee, C. (1996). *Music at the edge: The music therapy experiences of a musician with AIDS.* London: Routledge.

Loewy, J. (Ed.). (1997). *Music therapy and pediatric pain.* Cherry Hill, NJ: Jeffrey Books.

Maranto. C. D. (Ed.). (1993). *Music therapy: International perspectives.* Pipersville, PA: Jeffrey Books.

Maranto, C. D. (1995). Reviewing the literature. In Barbara L. Wheeler (Ed.), *Music therapy research: Quantitative and qualitative perspectives* (pp. 197–209). Phoenixville, PA: Barcelona Publishers.

McGuire, M. G. (1995). Writing the research report. In Barbara L. Wheeler (Ed.), *Music therapy research: Quantitative and qualitative perspectives* (pp. 261–279). Phoenixville, PA: Barcelona Publishers.

Nordoff, P., & Robbins, C. (1971). *Therapy in music for handicapped children.* London: Victor Gollancz.

Nordoff, P., & Robbins, C. (1977). *Creative music therapy.* New York: John Day & Co.

Pavlicevic, M. (1997). *Music therapy in context: Music, meaning, and relationship.* London and Philadelphia: Jessica Kingsley Publishers.

Pavlicevic, M. (1999). *Music therapy: Intimate notes.* London and Philadelphia: Jessica Kingsley Publishers.

Ritholz, M. S., & Turry, A. (1994). The journey by train: Creative music therapy with a 17-year-old boy. *Music Therapy, 12*(2), 58–87.

Robbins, C. M., & Robbins, C. (1991). Self-communications in creative music therapy. In Kenneth E. Bruscia (Ed.), *Case studies in music therapy* (pp. 55–72). Gilsum, NH: Barcelona Publishers.

Skewes, K. (2001). *The experience of group music therapy for six bereaved adolescents.* Unpublished doctoral dissertation, University of Melbourne.

Soshensky, R. (2001). Music therapy and addiction. *Music Therapy Perspectives, 19*(1), 45–52.

Stake, G. (1978). The case study method in social inquiry. *Educational Researcher, 7*, 5–8.

Stephens, G. (1981). Adele: A study in silence. *Music Therapy, 1,* 25–31.

Strunk, W., Jr., & White, E. B. (2000). *The elements of style* (4th ed.). Needham Heights, MA: Allyn & Bacon.

Summer, L. & Nolan, P. (Eds.). (2001). The role of music in the music therapy process [Special issue.]. *Music Therapy Perspectives, 19*(1).

Taylor, D.B. (1997). *Biomedical foundations of music as therapy.* St. Louis, MO: MMB Music, Inc.

Turabian, K. L. (1987). *A manual for writers of term papers, theses, and dissertations.* Chicago: University of Chicago Press.

University of Chicago Press. (1993). *The Chicago manual of style* (14th ed.). Chicago: Author.

Wheeler, B. L. (1995a). *Music therapy research: Quantitative and qualitative perspectives*. Phoenixville, PA: Barcelona Publishers.

Wheeler, B. L. (1995b). Developing a topic. In Barbara L. Wheeler (Ed.), *Music therapy research: Quantitative and qualitative perspectives* (pp. 183–194). Phoenixville, PA: Barcelona Publishers.

Wolcott, H. F. (1990). *Writing up qualitative research.* Newbury Park. CA: Sage Publications.

# Author Index

# Subject Index